Hoosier Hitmen

Indiana University Baseball

Indiana had never won a Big Ten baseball championship until coach Everett Dean arrived in 1925. He changed that in his first season by winning the title with a 9-2 record, 12-6 overall. This was quite an achievement considering IU had gone 12-25-1 in its previous three seasons. Dean is pictured on the back row, far left.

Nobody left as big a mark on Indiana University sports in the first half of the 20th Century as much as Zora Clevenger. He was a standout shortstop in the early 1900s. He also played basketball and football. Clevenger was IU's first football All-American, winning the honor as a center in 1903. He was the head baseball and basketball coach in 1905 and '06. He later was the Hoosier athletic director from 1923 to 1946. During his tenure, Indiana won its first Big Ten football championship (1945), three league baseball titles, three conference basketball crowns, and the 1940 national basketball championship.

HOOSIER HITMEN

Indiana University Baseball

Pete DiPrimio

ARCADIA
PUBLISHING

ISBN 978-0-7385-3196-0

Published by Arcadia Publishing
Charleston, South Carolina

Printed in the United States of America

Library of Congress Catalog Card Number: Applied For

For all general information contact Arcadia Publishing at:
Telephone 843-853-2070
Fax 843-853-0044
E-mail sales@arcadiapublishing.com
For customer service and orders:
Toll-Free 1-888-313-2665

Visit us on the Internet at www.arcadiapublishing.com

IU baseball began on this field, located in what is now known as Seminary Park in the block surrounded by First, Second, College, and Walnut streets just south of the downtown square. Back then it was called Seminary Field or the University Athletic Field. It was in use until 1898, when Jordan Field was built. This photo shows action from the May 30, 1892 Intercollegiate Championship game between Indiana and DePauw. IU won 13-11.

Contents

ACKNOWLEDGMENTS

Had woodshed time arrived? Was the summons to Assembly Hall's fourth floor storage room, which meant climbing concrete stairs well suited for inducing cardiac arrest, a sign that Indiana University's sports information staff had finally tired of me?

It wasn't, of course, and for that I am grateful. The windowless room contained enough Indiana baseball information and photos to guarantee this project's success.

Hoosier Hitmen is the culmination of much labor and love, doubt and belief, frustration and satisfaction. Without the effort of a lot of generous people, it would never have been completed.

IU assistant athletic director/media relations Jeff Fanter paved the way by allowing access to his department's many files and photos. He saved me time, money, and many sleepless nights.

Christy Tolin, assistant media relations director, bore the brunt of my non-stop requests and various screwups with a smile. She was accommodating despite my many interruptions of her hectic schedule. She assisted with photos, photo scanning, interviews and a whole host of behind-the-scenes necessities. There were times I'm certain she wanted to strangle me. That she didn't is something I'll always appreciate.

IU coach Bob Morgan was a deciding factor. He provided the necessary push to ensure this book's completion. He entertained me with stories and enlightened me with insight from 20 years in charge of the program. It's easy to understand why he's been so successful for so long.

Assistant media relations director Beth Feickert was there in a big way for old photos, access to secret files and the wonders of photo scanning. And when I occasionally talked to myself, she understood.

Jeff Smith, former media relations staff assistant, braved Assembly Hall's daunting steps to take me to the fourth floor, down to the basement for a visit with IU photographer Paul Riley, and then back to the fourth floor. Both our knowledge of Hoosier baseball, and our fitness, benefited.

Gavin Lang, assistant media relations director, provided use of his cubicle and friendly expertise as I scanned photos. Todd Starowitz, assistant media relations director, offered the perspective and humor I often needed. Former staff assistants Amy DiMico and Lindsay Carpenter listened even while busy with their own tasks.

And then there were the dozens of baseball managers who compiled records, pasted photographs, and cut out newspaper clippings to provide yearly insights into the program.

I'd very much like to thank assistant coach Jeff Calcaterra and former Hoosier coaches and players who added human interest to all the numbers and statistics that dominate so much of baseball.

I have to mention Arcadia acquisitions editor Jeff Ruetsche, who provided answers to my many questions. He was great to work with.

I can't forget my children, Gabrielle and Vincent, who tried, sometimes successfully, to stay out of my office as I worked. Still, Vince always had questions—some of which I could answer—and Gabrielle always offered hugs—all of which I needed.

And finally, there is my wife, Cindy. She is strong and resilient and passionate, attributes I very much need. Without her love and support, this project would never have been finished.

INTRODUCTION

Baseball matters.

Even amidst Indiana University's vast basketball shadow, the crack of bats and the flash of cleats signify something special.

"Baseball should be very good at Indiana," athletic director Terry Clapacs said. "We're the southernmost Big Ten school. We have a longer playing season than the other Big Ten schools. Baseball has always been a popular sport in Indiana. We want to be very competitive in the Big Ten."

And so a new stadium will someday rise in the intramural fields northeast of Assembly Hall. It will be well designed, state-of-the-art and fan friendly. Assembly Hall should be so lucky.

Baseball will never rival basketball in stirring Cream 'n Crimson passion. Roundball roots run too deep; Hoosier Hysteria's hold is too strong. And yet, baseball is the university's oldest sport. It fielded teams just as the Civil War ended (1865). Union Army veterans, who played the sport as recreation during the war, probably were among IU's first players.

Indiana didn't start keeping records until 1896, didn't officially begin Big Ten competition until 1906. Early on, games were few and successes inconsistent. In the 29 seasons before coach Everett Dean's 1925 arrival, the Hoosiers had 13 winning records. They had 12 in Dean's 14 seasons and won the school's first three conference titles.

Coach Paul Harrell maintained a winning pace through the 1940s before Ernie Andres took charge for his 24-year run. Indiana struggled for most of the 1970s until Larry Smith started a rejuvenation program and Bob Morgan accelerated it with a series of 40-plus victory seasons, highlighted by a 57-19-1 mark in 1985.

IU baseball produced memorable men who shaped the future of the university and the country. William Lowe Bryan was a second baseman on the 1884 team. He went on to become IU president from 1902–1937. He helped build the school into one of the nation's major universities and committed Indiana into full Big Ten academic and athletic integration.

Sherman "Shay" Minton was a baseball and football standout in 1912 and 1913. The IU Law School graduate became a U.S. senator and a U.S. Supreme Court justice. Paul McNutt took his baseball roots into political prominence. He became governor of Indiana. In 1940, he was the favorite to become the Democratic candidate for president until Franklin Roosevelt decided to break tradition by running for a third term. A dormitory complex is named after him.

Lloyd Balfour was a first baseman who became a successful jewelry manufacturer and generous university donor. A yearly university award is named after him.

IU baseball produced major league players who made a difference.

Ted Kluszewski was a Hoosier baseball and football standout in the mid-1940s, a slugging first baseman for the Cincinnati Reds in the 1950s. For four seasons, from 1953-56, he was the National League's most fearsome slugger, the Barry Bonds of his era. In that span he hit 171 home runs, drove in 464 runs and never batted below .302, making the All-Star team each year. He just missed the 1954 Triple Crown, leading the league in home runs (49) and runs batted in (141) and finishing fifth in hitting (.326—Willie Mays won at .345).

Mickey Morandini was a National League All-Star second baseman for the Philadelphia Phillies in 1995. He played 10 years in the majors and finished with a .268 career batting average.

Highlights included playing in the 1993 World Series and helping to spark the Chicago Cubs to a rare postseason appearance in 1998.

John Wehner, now a minor league coach in the Pittsburgh Pirates organization, was a popular Pirate utility player in the 1990s. He hit over .300 three times, with a high of .340 as a rookie in 1991.

Kevin Orie played with the Chicago Cubs, Florida Marlins, and Philadelphia Phillies from 1997 to 2002. The utility third baseman was a career .249 hitter.

IU baseball produced college players who dominated the competition. Mike Smith had one of the greatest college seasons of all-time in 1992, when he led the nation in batting (.490), home runs (27) and runs batted in (95). At one point during that season, he hit nine home runs in nine days.

Don Ritter was the Hoosiers' first All-America, winning the honor in 1949. He batted (.439 in league play, .393 overall) and pitched (2-0) Indiana to the Big Ten championship.

Pitcher Jerry Dill had a ridiculously low 0.36 earned run average in league competition in 1964. Twelve Indiana hitters have led the conference in batting since official statistics began being kept in 1939.

The 1949 Big Ten championship was one of five Indiana has won over the years. The first three came under Dean (1925, '32, and '38). Dean also was a successful IU basketball coach who won three conference titles before going to Stanford. His Stanford team won the 1942 NCAA Tournament basketball championship.

Andres, a former two-sport Hoosier standout who played professional baseball and basketball, guided the Hoosiers to the 1949 crown. As a rookie coach he turned around a team that had gone 3-9 in conference competition the previous year. That earned IU a short-lived NCAA tourney opportunity. The Hoosiers were eliminated in their opening game, losing 8-3 to Western Michigan in their first NCAA tournament appearance.

Indiana's next NCAA shot came 47 years later. The 1996 Hoosiers, having finished second in the Big Ten during the regular season, earned an automatic NCAA bid by winning the league tournament title. That included three grueling games with Illinois. IU won the first 6-3, lost the second 8-5 and won the finale 6-4. Playing in the NCAA Midwest Regional in Wichita, Kansas, the Hoosiers opened with top-ranked Wichita State and lost 4-0. They recorded their first ever NCAA victory by beating Delaware 10-8, then were eliminated with an 11-8 loss to Rice and future Houston Astros All-Star Lance Berkman.

That Indiana squad was guided by Bob Morgan, the winningest coach in school history and one of the winningest coaches in college history. Entering the 2004 season he had 1,019 victories in his 28-year career, 727 at Indiana.

"Coach Morgan and I still talk," Mike Smith said, "and when we do, we do nothing but laugh. That's what makes it so special. He was tough. He was difficult. But I wouldn't trade it for anything. What he put me through, what the program put me through, what I gained from that, is something I still use today."

One

Hoosier Hitmen

Triple Crown Glory

For one season, Mike Smith hit like no Division I player had before. He hit for average and power. He hit when runners filled the bases and when they did not. He hit balls so hard and so often in 1992 you wondered if he'd ever make an out.

"He just got on a roll," coach Bob Morgan said. "He competed so hard. He was such a tough out."

When Smith was finished, he had set school records for average (.490), home runs (27) and runs batted in (95). He led the nation in all three categories, plus slugging percentage (.760), to cap a monster season despite non-monster size.

"He wasn't a big, intimidating player," former IU catcher and current Hoosier assistant coach Jeff Calcaterra said. "He wasn't even the best player on the team. Kevin Orie was by far the more talented player. But Mike was the best production guy I ever saw."

Flash back to April 19, 1992. The Hoosiers were poised to win the final three games of a four-game series at Michigan—if they could overcome a 7-2 deficit in the final game.

"It was one of the most remarkable things I've ever seen in baseball," Calcaterra said. "We're down 7-2 in a seven-inning game. In the fifth Mike hits a three-run homer and as he comes back to the dugout he said 'Get me up one more time.' Well, we get to the seventh and we're down 8-5. There's a guy on and Rich Vozel walks on a 3-2 pitch to get to Mike."

Michigan brought in reliever Todd Marion, a hard-throwing sidearm pitcher who had led the Big Ten in saves that season.

"He throws two sliders and makes Mike look ugly," Calcaterra said. "On the third pitch he threw another slider and Mike parked it over the left field wall."

That tied the game. IU won 9-8 in extra innings.

By his junior year, Smith was a star. He won the Big Ten batting title with a .472 average (.431 overall). He slugged 15 home runs.

"That year he came out of nowhere," Calcaterra said. Major league teams didn't care. Nobody drafted him. "He thought he should have been drafted, so the next year he doubled his production."

"I wanted to prove some people wrong," Smith said. He did in a big way.

"The thing about Smitty was he learned how to handle his emotions and how to handle failure," Morgan said. "Early in his career he didn't handle it well. He'd be too hard on himself. He was still hard on himself, but he didn't fail that much, so he didn't have to deal with it much."

Despite a back injury, Smith started strong his senior season and never slumped.

"I had to wear a back brace and I was concerned about being able to swing the bat," he said, "but I got through it and got through it with power." Smith's power surge broke Bill Mueller's school homer record of 23. "I'd gotten stronger. I'd committed to the weights. And I got hot in the Big Ten."

Smith's exploits generated national attention. *Baseball Weekly* and *Baseball America* kept track of his Triple Crown run. *Sports Illustrated* mentioned him in its Faces in the Crowd section. And after beating out Cal State Fullerton's Phil Nevin (.402, 22 HR, 86 RBIs) and Maryland's Derick Hacopian (.421, 23 HR, 84 RBIs) for the Triple Crown, *The Sporting News* named him national player of the year.

"He hit everything and he always hit in good counts because he had good discipline," Calcaterra said. "He saw the ball well. He had good hands and wrists that allowed him to hit."

"He had good talent," Morgan said, "but he was somewhat of an overachiever. For him to do what he did is remarkable for a kid from a Midwest school."

Smith's Ted Williams' impression flamed out against pro pitching. He never made it past Triple-A ball.

"It didn't click for me early on like I needed it to," he said. "I didn't capitalize on the opportunity, which stings me more than anything."

Smith was a fifth-round draft choice of the Texas Rangers in 1992 and was sent to Gastonia, South Carolina, in Class A. He wanted a fast start for a fast impression. Instead, he had the worst start imaginable.

"As a college senior draftee, you need to announce your presence with authority because you're older," he said. "But I started 0-for-18. It easily could have been 12-for-18, but it wasn't and I started to change some things. I had a manager who tried to screw with my swing. No excuses. I didn't adjust to all the changes he was doing to my swing. Then it snowballed and I never got out. I lost power and the ability to drive the ball."

With Class A ball filled with younger prospects, Smith felt the pressure.

"Because you're older, you lose the luster real quick as a prospect if you don't get out of the gate fast in a low Class A league," he said. "If I had started off with a bang, things might have been different."

Smith had a solid year at Tulsa (.270 average, 16 home runs) in double-A, and was promoted to triple-A, but that's where it ended. Lacking experience to play shortstop—"I felt I could have been a utility player in the majors, but you really need to play short and I didn't have that experience professionally"—Smith accepted a front office job with the Rangers.

"Was it emotional to quit? No. It was hard to give up on a dream, but my next goal was to be a general manager of a major league club."

After three years as the Rangers' assistant farm director, Smith left for graduate school at the University of Texas-Arlington. He now runs sales and operations for Cypress Communications in Dallas.

"I'll always look at my experience at IU as much greater than my professional experience," he said. "What the program and the school taught me, what I took from it, is what I apply in the business world. It provided me a great foundation for life after baseball."

Baseball Hercules

Ted Kluszewski was Mark McGwire before there was Mark McGwire. He was the precursor to Harmon Killebrew, Willie McCovey and Frank Howard and all the other NFL-sized men who smashed their way to stardom in the 1960s.

The left-handed hitting first baseman batted .298 with 279 home runs and 1,028 runs batted in during an injury hindered 15-year major league career. During his final five seasons he was a pinch hitter nearly as much as a starter. Still, he batted over .300 seven times and led National League first baseman in fielding five straight years, a major league record.

He even was a fashion maker as the Cincinnati Reds went to sleeveless uniforms to accommodate his bulging biceps. He was called "Strong Man" and "Baseball Hercules" and "Big Klu." He was "mighty" and "bruising" and his strength inspired legends. For instance, there's the story of a fight between the Reds and Cardinals. One Cardinal, Solly Hemus, was running to join the fray when Kluszewski lifted him off the ground.

"Where are you going?" Kluszewski asked.

"Nowhere, Ted," the 5-foot-9, 175-pound Hemus said.

Then there was the time then New York Giants manager Leo Durocher listed baseball's strongest players and left off Kluszewski. Asked why, Durocher said, "I'm talking about human beings."

Finally, NL umpire Larry Goetz once said Kluszewski hit the ball so hard he could kill a person OUTSIDE Crosley Field, Cincinnati's home ballpark. He said this after seeing Kluszewski smash a line drive off a building across Western Avenue from the stadium.

Indiana had never seen a baseball player like Kluszewski. For one thing, he was a football player, an end on the Hoosiers' unbeaten 1945 Big Ten champions. He was 6-foot-2 and 225 pounds, a giant in those times.

Kluszewski was an all-Big Ten football player in 1945, joining teammates Pete Phios, Bob Ravensberg and George Taliaferro. Ravensberg was the other end and he went on to earn first team All-America honors, catching 12 passes for 128 yards and five touchdowns. Kluszewski caught 10 passes, including one for a touchdown, and ran once for five yards. He also had a 56-yard punt and scored three touchdowns.

Still, Kluszewski's biggest impact came during his one year of Hoosier baseball. He was a power-hitting center fielder capable of knocking balls well beyond the boundaries of Jordan Field, located at what is now the parking lot next to the Memorial Union. Although coming from fast-pitch softball roots (he was a standout sandlot player in his hometown of Argo, Illinois) Kluszewski quickly adapted. Adaptation was helped by Jordan Field's short right field. Seventh Street was about 230 feet from home plate.

"A good left-handed hitter loved it," said Ernie Andres, who played right field for the Hoosiers in the late 1930s. "It was a good field for a guy like Kluszewski."

In his first game, an exhibition against the Indianapolis Indians of the American Association, Kluszewski went 1-for-4 with an infield single. But his first official display of power came in an April 7 victory over visiting Michigan State. His two-run, two-out home run—the ball carried to the lawn of the IU Business School—produced a 7-5 win. It was his third hit of the game. He added a stolen base and drove in three runs.

Bob Dro, himself a former two-sport Hoosier athlete (baseball and basketball), remembers seeing Kluszewski bounce balls off what was then called The Fieldhouse, the basketball arena. It is now called Wildemuth Intramural Center and is nearly 500 feet from where home plate used to be.

"Oh my could he hit," Dro said. "He hit a ball up against the building we were playing basketball in. He hit it over the over the road (7th Street) to The Fieldhouse. He was a big guy and a great hitter."

Kluszewski hit .443 in the spring of 1945, .433 in Big Ten play, drove in 10 runs, had 21 assists from the outfield, and earned the attention of Cincinnati scouts. Because of the war, teams didn't go to Florida for spring training. Instead, they worked out closer to their home cities and the Reds chose Bloomington.

The Reds offered Kluszewski a $15,000 signing bonus in December of 1945 and he took it. Andres, who played minor league ball in the Boston Red Sox organization before becoming the long-time IU coach, met Kluszewski in an exhibition game in Tampa, Florida, in the spring of 1946.

"You could see he was a pretty good hitter," Andres said. "He was a dangerous hitter. He could really hurt you with the bat. At that time, the Reds didn't know whether to put him in the outfield or first base. They sent him to Columbia, South Carolina, gave him a first baseman's mitt and that's where he ended up playing. He became a pretty good first baseman."

Kluszewski made instant impact, batting .352 in 1946 to lead the South Atlantic League. He hit .377 in 1947 to lead the Southern Association.

Kluszewski played his first major league game at age 22 (making $10,000) in 1947, his last at 36 in 1961. By the time he was 31, he had 245 home runs and was a few more good years away from making a serious run at 500. Then injuries struck, playing time dwindled and he hit just 34 more homers the rest of his career.

"If he had stayed healthy," Andres said, "who knows what he could have done."

It took Kluszewski three seasons to find his major league rhythm. By 1950, he was a star, smacking 25 home runs in a sign of things to come.

From 1953–56, he was one of the National League's most feared players. In 1953 he hit .316 with 40 homers and 108 RBIs. In 1954 it was .326, 49, and 141. In 1955 it was .314, 47, and 113. In 1956, it was .302, 35, and 102. The 49 homers were a Reds record until George Foster belted 52 in 1977.

In 1954, Kluszewski broke Johnny Mize's National League record by scoring a run in 17 straight games. A year later, he led the league in hits, with 192.

Then it all slipped away. He was traded to the Pittsburgh Pirates in 1957, struggled and was traded to the Chicago White Sox in August of 1959, joining another former Hoosier, Sam Esposito. He reaped the benefits by helping the White Sox to the American League pennant and ending a New York Yankee dynasty that had produced nine pennants in the previous 10 years.

Kluszewski made the most of his only World Series, hitting .391 with three home runs and a World Series six-game record of 10 RBIs. He opened with a bang, slugging two homers and driving in five runs in Chicago's 11-0 first game victory over the Los Angeles Dodgers.

Los Angeles went on to win the series four games to two. The Dodgers won Game Six, 9-3, despite Kluszewski's three-run homer. After the Series, each White Sox received $7,272. The winning Dodgers received $11,231 a man.

Kluszewski's final national moment came amid controversy on August 28, 1960, when his three-run homer off Baltimore's Milt Pappas was disallowed. Umpire Ed Hurley had called time just before Pappas threw the pitch. The eighth-inning homer would have tied the score at 3. After 15 fruitless minutes of arguing by the White Sox's Nellie Fox and Al Lopez—both were ejected—Kluszewski batted again and lined out. The Orioles won 3-1.

Kluszewski, who never made more than $40,000 in a season, also played for the California Angels before retiring after the 1961 season. His final public power show came on February 20, 1971, when he smacked a 500-foot single—yes, a single—that drove in three runs and led the NL to a 5-3 win over the AL in the annual March of Dimes old-timers' game.

Kluszewski later coached for Cincinnati. He was the hitting coach for the 1976 Big Red Machine. He died on March 28, 1988.

"Boy he had some great years," Dro said. "He was just a good guy."

THE MIGHTY MICK

In the end, a bad right shoulder betrayed Mickey Morandini. It joined the list of failed body parts—Sandy Koufax's left elbow, Bo Jackson's left hip, Don Mattingly's back—that have ended major league careers.

"I've got severe arthritis in my throwing shoulder and it forced me to retire," the former National League All-Star second baseman said. "It keeps me from doing things because of the pain."

Morandini's post major league athletic ventures center on working with his three sons in Little League baseball.

"Once in a while I play in a basketball or softball league, but nothing too extensive," he said.

Retirement finds Morandini helping with his wife's Chesterton, Indiana, invitation business. The Morandinis built a home in the northwestern Indiana community while he was with the Chicago Cubs (and making $2 million a year).

"We do weddings, baby announcements, parties, stuff like that," he said. "I do all the printing and behind-the-scenes stuff."

Morandini was 34 when his career ended with the suddenness of a Roger Clemens fastball. He had played for Philadelphia and Toronto in the 2000 season, hitting a combined .257 with 29 runs batted in. His defense was solid as usual (he finished with a .989 career fielding percentage). He reported for spring training in 2001 with a sore shoulder, but no indication of what was coming.

"I had no problems in 2000," he said. "Then I went to spring training and I wasn't feeling right. I had a MRI and found out I had a torn rotator cuff and some arthritis. I had surgery, but the arthritis got worse and worse." His playing options dwindled to zero. "There was nothing I could do about it."

Morandini finished with a career .268 average, 32 home runs, and 351 runs batted in. He hit as many as 40 doubles, stole as many as 26 bases. His best season was 1998, when he set career highs in average (.296), homers (8) and RBIs (53). That was in his first season in Chicago after being traded by Philadelphia for pitcher Doug Glanville.

The next year Morandini averaged just .241. His refusal to sign a contract extension resulted in reduced playing time and a certainty he wouldn't be back.

Then it was back to Philadelphia and his professional roots. He played with the Phillies for his first seven seasons. That included the 1993 National League playoffs (he hit .250), the '93 World Series (he hit .200), and the '95 All-Star Game. He became close friends with pitcher Curt Schilling, who later became a World Series hero with the Arizona Diamondbacks.

Morandini entered the record books in 1992 when he recorded the first unassisted triple play in 65 years. It came against the Pittsburgh Pirates. With Andy Van Slyke on second and Barry Bonds on first, Jeff King hit a line drive up the middle. Morandini made a diving catch, then tagged Bonds and stepped on second to get Van Slyke.

"From a personal aspect the biggest thrill I had was the All-Star Game," he said. "But the most special was playing in the World Series. It's the reason you play. Not a lot of players get to do it."

Morandini's chance to do it came after an impressive four years at Indiana. He earned all-conference honors in 1986, '87, and '88 by excelling at all phases of the game. He hit a team-leading .422 as a sophomore in 1986 and never slowed down.

"Mickey was a mentally tough kid," coach Bob Morgan said. "A quiet kid. You never knew if anything was wrong. He just competed. He didn't make waves. You knew what to expect from him every day."

Morandini's .383 career batting average ranks fourth in school history. His 186 runs batted in are third. His 127 steals, 127 extra base hits, and 277 runs are first.

"I was always a good contact hitter and a fast runner," he said. "Occasionally I'd hit a home run, but I wasn't a big, strong power guy." Perhaps not, but his 37 career home runs rank fourth in school history. "That's what they call the aluminum advantage. I could hit the ball with some pop and those aluminum bats make the ball go further than normal."

Still, his preference remains wood, which is what they use at the professional level.

"There's the old saying that once you use wood, you never want to go back to aluminum," he said. "You hit a ball solid with wood and there's no better feeling."

Morandini played during the most offense-oriented time of the coach Bob Morgan era. From 1985–88, the Hoosiers never hit less than .303 or averaged fewer than 7.5 runs a game. They hit .355 in 1988, .344 in 1985. They scored a school-record 636 runs in '85 en route to a school-record 57 victories. That team included Bill Mueller, Alex Smith, and Mike Sabo, all of whom are well represented on the school record lists.

"We had a lot of good offensive players," Morandini said. "We had some real good teams. But we got into situations where our good pitchers ran into some arm trouble. We were always right in the middle of things in the Big Ten. We were right on the edge of making [the Big Ten] tournament, but we never did."

Morandini came to IU out of western Pennsylvania (as did teammate and future major leaguer John Wehner). He chose the Hoosiers over Iowa, a decision made easy in part because of his appreciation for basketball. He once said that his best Indiana memory was the Hoosiers winning the 1987 national basketball championship.

"I'm a big Bobby Knight fan," he said.

And when his Hoosier run was over, Morandini got one final amateur thrill by playing on the 1988 U.S. Olympic team. Although an exhibition sport at the time, the U.S. won the gold medal. Teammates included pitchers Jim Abbott, Andy Benes, and Ben McDonald, plus third baseman Robin Ventura.

"We had a solid team," Morandini said. "A lot of guys had good major league careers."

That Morandini is included on that list (earning almost $10 million in his final six seasons), he said, is due to what he learned at Indiana.

"The four years there were by far the most I improved as a player," he said. "It was hard. We worked our butts off. But it was a fun place to play."

Triple Crown Suprise

Mike Smith wasn't the first Hoosier to win the Big Ten Triple Crown. In 1958, Bob Lawrence, who would go on to coach IU in the 1970s, became the first player to ever lead the league in hitting (.472), home runs (5) and runs batted in (14). Not bad for someone who only played college baseball one season.

"He was a natural hitter," former IU coach Ernie Andres said. "He had a lot of power. He was just a powerful guy."

Much of that power came from his football background. An all-state player out of Beaver Falls, Pennsylvania, Lawrence played football his first two years in Bloomington before going out for baseball as a left-handed hitting first baseman.

"The idea was I could play baseball and not have to go to spring practice," he said.

As it turned out, Lawrence missed more than spring football. He never played the sport again after the Boston Red Sox offered what was then a huge signing bonus of $50,000 in the summer of 1958.

"The average salary back then was about $4,000," Lawrence said. "I had a pretty good year and you never know if you'll have another one or not. And back then, they didn't have a draft, so you went with whoever offered you the most money. The Red Sox offered the most, so I signed."

Lawrence never made the majors, although he did have one memorable minor league season for double-A Seattle—30 home runs, 127 runs batted in. His development was hurt because of a year in the service in 1961.

"I wasn't close to making it to the majors," he said. "I was hanging on at triple-A."

By 1965, Lawrence's pro career was over. He returned to IU to work on his masters and Andres offered him an assistant coaching job.

"We had a good working relationship," Lawrence said. "And when Ernie retired, the IU job fell into my hands."

Lawrence's playing-and-coaching career included the switch from wood to aluminum bats in the early 1970s.

"Once colleges went to aluminum," he said, "the hitting really picked up. That was the biggest change in the game."

The switch helped offset the cost of replacing wood bats, which were breaking at a high rate.

"The version we heard was that Louisville (Louisville Slugger, the company that made wood bats for the pros as well as high schools and colleges) was getting scarce on wood," Lawrence said. "They were shipping all the good wood to the pro teams and we were getting second-rate wood. It broke almost every time you swung the bat. So they came up with this aluminum bat and they keep improving on it. The ball jumps off it pretty well. You could miss-hit a ball and still get better distance than you would with wood. The sweet spot was a little bigger and you could just hit it harder and farther."

Big Ten Batting Bests

While Barry Burnett never won a Triple Crown, he did best future major league All-Star Dave Winfield. As a senior in 1973, Burnett led the Big Ten with a .471 average, clinching the title with a pair of hits in the season's last game off of Winfield, who dominated as a pitcher and a hitter. Winfield finished second with a .453 average.

Don Ritter, whose nickname was "Tex," thrived in basketball as well as baseball. As a senior, he scored 26 points against Notre Dame in basketball, and then helped the Hoosiers to the 1949 Big Ten baseball title by winning the league batting crown with a .439 average, one point better than Ohio State's Bob Weygant. He was IU's first baseball All-American.

"He was about as good a hitter as I ever had," Andres said. "He could hit left and righthanders just as well."

Outfielder Bobby Robertson led the Big Ten in hitting with a .438 average en route to an all-conference season in 1954. He also was a standout football player.

"If he had played baseball through college, he might have been great," Andres said. "He could hit it out of sight. He could run. He was a good base runner and a good fielder. I know he played football, but he had a baseball heart."

Another league batting champion was Eddie LaDuke. The second baseman hit .431 in Big Ten play in 1962, but because of struggles in non-conference play, finished at .319 overall. Although not a large player (5-foot-6 and 165 pounds), he hit 10 career home runs. He hit .353 as a junior.

Other Hoosier Big Ten batting champs were Jack Campbell (.381 in 1966), Scott Weiner (.453 in 1976), Bill Jordan (.431 in 1989), Matt Braughler (.444 in 1996), and Vasili Spanos (.434 in 2003).

Spanos is the latest Hoosier to earn a shot at professional glory. Oakland selected him in the 11th round of the 2003 draft after a stellar senior season in which he led the Big Ten in hitting, home runs (8), on-base percentage (.525) and slugging percentage (.778). His league batting average was 40 points higher than the Big Ten's next-best hitter. Overall he hit .412 with 47 RBIs and 11 home runs—not bad for someone who played the final two weeks with a broken left hand.

In four seasons as the starting third baseman, Spanos had a career batting average of .365, which ranks in the top 10 in school history, and a .673 slugging percentage, the second-best ever by a Hoosier. He tied for third with 43 career homers and ranks sixth with 228 hits, fifth with 51 doubles, and fifth with 100 extra-base hits. His 185 RBIs tie him with Mike Smith for third.

Not bad for a former walk-on.

"We got Vasili after I saw him in a Chicago all-star game," Calcaterra said. "It was in June after his high school senior year and he wasn't going anywhere. We didn't have any money available, so he was a recruited walk-on. He played as a freshman."

In fact, Spanos started as a freshman. Morgan wanted to give him a partial scholarship, but Spanos' father, George, told him to use the money for a pitcher.

Spanos, the son of Greek immigrants, has thrived despite being diagnosed with diabetes when he was nine years old. He has to take daily insulin injections.

"He's just a great kid," Morgan said. "He had a remarkable career."

Special Mention

Sammy Esposito wasn't a big-time hitter at IU—he batted just .252 with two home runs and 12 RBIs in 1952, his only season after a standout football career—but he played in the majors for 10 years with the Chicago White Sox after getting a signing bonus of $50,000.

A utility player who played shortstop, second base, third base, and the outfield, Esposito had a career batting average of .207. His best season came in 1956 when he hit .228 with three home runs and 25 RBIs. He played in the 1959 World Series, going 0-for-2 with one strikeout.

"He got the furthest of any guy I coached," Andres said.

Shortstop Jim Deneff earned All-America honors in 1966, a year in which he hit .354 and led the Hoosiers in doubles (11), home runs (4), total bases (62), and slugging percentage (.549).

Catcher Ken St. Pierre made All-American in 1974 when he hit .313 with six home runs and 39 RBIs. He also committed just two errors in 104 chances.

Second baseman Dan Haegele made honorable mention All-American in 1998 when he hit .323 with a team-leading 15 stolen bases.

IU coaches were counting on outfielder Kennard Jones to be a two-year starter after signing him out of junior college. But in his first season, in 2002, he was the Big Ten's tri-player of the year when he hit .404 with 75 runs, 33 RBIs, and 22 steals. That attracted major league scouts and he was a third round draft choice of the San Diego Padres.

"He was like Mike Smith," coach Bob Morgan said. "He was a mentally tough kid who could really hit."

Morgan lists Kevin Orie as the most talented player he ever had. Orie led IU in almost every hitting category in 1993 to earn all-conference honors. He finished with a .357 career batting average, 34 homers (including 20 in 1992), and 151 runs batted in. He played in the major leagues for six seasons.

"He was a tough kid," Morgan said. "Injuries hurt him most of his career, but he's probably the best athlete I ever had."

Mike Smith dominated college baseball like few players ever have in 1991 and '92. He peaked in '92 by winning the national Triple Crown, a feat that has never been equaled in NCAA Division I play. He led the nation in batting average (.490), home runs (27) and runs batted in (95). All are school records. Overall, Smith owns 10 IU Big Ten season batting records.

Mike Smith is tied with Mike Sabo for the Indiana school career home run record. Both had 47. Smith had only five home runs after his first two seasons, then hit 42 in his final two.

Ted Kluszewski played only one year of baseball at Indiana, but he made it count. The left-handed-hitting outfielder hit .443 in 1945, the second-highest average in school history. He signed later that year with the Cincinnati Reds for $15,000. He went on to become one of the major league's top home run hitters in the mid-1950s, with a high of 49 in 1954.

Ted Kluszewski was a two-sport standout. In football he made all-conference at end in 1945. He and fellow end Bob Ravensberg, who earned All-Big Ten and All-America honors, were a potent pair as the Hoosiers went 9-0-1 that season and won the conference championship. The 7-7 tie came at Northwestern.

Mickey Morandini is all over the IU record books. He has the school single-season record for runs (90) and slugging percentage (.844). He's the career leader in triples (29), runs (277), stolen bases (127) and extra base hits (127). He also ranks second in career hits (299) and shares the career lead in doubles (61) with Alex Smith. He played from 1985–88.

Third baseman Vasili Spanos thrived at the plate from the moment he arrived on campus as a preferred walk-on in the fall of 1999. He hit a team-leading .358 as a freshman, slugged a team-leading 11 home runs as a sophomore and earned All-American honors as a junior while hitting .385 with 16 home runs and 65 runs batted in. He capped his outstanding career in 2003 by leading the Big Ten in hitting as a senior at .434. His on-base percentage of .525 ranked third nationally. He was drafted in the 11th round by the Oakland As.

Kevin Orie was a dominant hitter for the Hoosiers in the early 1990s. He had a career batting average of .358, the 13th best mark in school history. His .668 career slugging percentage ranks second among IU players. He ranks sixth with 34 career home runs, including 20 in 1992. That's the third most in school history. Orie went on to play in the major leagues from 1997 to 2002. He was a utility player for the Chicago Cubs, Florida Marlins, and Philadelphia Phillies. He had a career batting average of .249 with 22 home runs and 116 runs batted in.

Mickey Morandini had a 10-year major league career as a second baseman for Philadelphia, Chicago, Texas, and Toronto. He played in the 1993 World Series while with the Phillies. His best season came in 1998 when he hit .296 with eight home runs and 53 runs batted in. He finished with a career .268 average, 32 home runs, and 351 RBIs.

John Wehner had one of the best hitting seasons in IU history in 1988, when he batted .436. That ranks fourth on the school's all-time list, behind Mike Smith (.490 in 1992), Ted Kluszewski (.443 in '45), and Bill Waite (.437 in '81). Wehner finished with a career batting average of .325.

John Wehner made the most of his pro opportunity, playing nine years as a utility player for the Pittsburgh Pirates and Florida Marlins in the 1990s. He hit .300 or better three times, with a high of .340 as a rookie in 1991 while playing in 37 games. That included a 5-for-5 game. His aggressive style made him a fan favorite even though he never played in more than 86 games or had more than 139 at bats in a season. He finished with a .249 career average, 4 home runs, and 54 runs batted in.

Mickey Morandini played on the 1988 U.S. Olympic team. Teammates included such future major league players as pitcher Jim Abbott and third baseman Robin Ventura. Two years later, he was with the Philadelphia Phillies. A torn rotator cuff on his right (throwing) shoulder led to arthritis that ended his career.

Mickey Morandini was a three-time all-conference choice, from 1986–88. His best power year came in 1986 when he hit 13 home runs, 10 triples and 22 doubles. His .844 slugging percentage that season remains the school record.

Alex Smith overcame a severe knee injury to become one of the all-time best hitters in Indiana history. His career batting average of .393 ranks second to Paul Harrell's .404 mark. He's also second in school career runs batted in with 223. He played from 1982–86.

In 1985 Alex Smith set the IU record for at bats in a season, with 242. No one has come within 15 at bats of that mark. He also has the school mark for most hits in a season, with 105 in 1985. He's the only Hoosier to ever record 100 hits in a season.

Bill Mueller is one of only three Hoosiers to hit at least 20 home runs in a season. He set the school record with 23 in 1985. That lasted for seven years until Mike Smith broke it with 27. Kevin Orie hit 20 home runs in 1992. Mueller drove in 87 runs in 1985, which is second in school history to Smith's 95 in 1992.

Mike Sabo was Indiana's top power hitter in the late 1980s. He slugged 47 career home runs to set the school record (Mike Smith tied it). He twice led the team in home runs, with 11 in 1987 and a career-high 14 in 1988.

Mike Sabo has the school record for runs batted in, with 231. The only other Hoosier over 200 is Alex Smith, with 223. Sabo's 120 career extra base hits are second to Mickey Morandini's 127.

Matt Braughler led the Big Ten in hitting in 1996, with a .444 average. That ranks as the fifth-best league mark in school history. His 23 career doubles in conference play tie Mickey Morandini for the school record.

Two

Those Championship Seasons

NCAA Debut

Even now, more than half a century later, Ernie Andres wonders. . . . If star pitcher Jim McGee had skipped his ill-fated shower, if he and his fellow Hoosiers had shown better judgment, Indiana might have made NCAA tourney noise in the spring of 1949.

Instead, you had the sound of silence that follows a season-ending defeat.

"He hurt his back in the shower," Andres said of McGee. "He was probably horsing around. I don't know. I never did know."

McGee's back injury cost him his curve ball—"the best of any pitcher I ever had," the coach said—and a start against Western Michigan in IU's first NCAA tourney appearance.

"He could really throw the curve," Andres said. "It dropped right off the cliff."

Without the curve, McGee was just a fastball pitcher and Andres didn't think that was enough. He also was without No. 2 pitcher Bill Tosheff, who Andres said, had "left for Alaska and a summer job."

That left Don Colnitis, whose 4-1 record and steady pitching made him the logical choice. But logic couldn't overcome bad defense. Five errors helped put IU in a 6-2 hole it couldn't overcome. IU lost 8-3.

McGee pitched the final three innings and didn't allow a run.

"I probably should have started McGee and just let him throw fastballs," said Andres, who still wonders about what could have been. "That was tough because I had two really tough pitchers in McGee and Tosheff."

Dynamic Debut

It was April of 1949 and Andres was a rookie head coach with a veteran team—as in war veteran. Five players had served in World War II and, because of the G.I. Bill, could afford college. That they also could play baseball was a bonus Andres exploited. Much of that was necessity—he hadn't done any recruiting.

Andres was still a player in the summer of 1948 and didn't arrive in Bloomington until that fall. By then he had no choice but to work with what talent he had. As it turned out, he had a lot.

"What really made that team was the G.I. Bill," he said. "They were a little older, like 24 or 25 years old, and were pretty good."

One of the oldest was Don Ritter, who first played for the Hoosiers in 1943. He hit just .158 while batting just 19 times that season. Then he left for the war and didn't return until 1947.

By 1949, Ritter was a dominating player. He was also a versatile one. He played basketball as did baseball teammates Gene Ring, Bill Stearman (who went on to win more than 700 games as an Indiana high school basketball coach), Tosheff and Lou Watson.

"I didn't have a problem getting basketball players to play," said Andres, who also was an assistant basketball coach. "Getting football players was tougher because of spring practice. Once in a while I'd get a guy who was a senior after his football was over.

"When John Pont came (Pont was the football coach from 1965–72) he would let them play if they wanted. He told me they'd better play. He didn't want them sitting on the bench with me."

Ritter was coming off an injury hindered junior season. A broken ankle had contributed to his .263 average. He came back in a big way in 1949. He won the Big Ten batting title while setting conference records for hits (25) and doubles (7). He also had a 2-0 record as a relief pitcher.

"He was probably the best player on that team," Andres said.

Ritter had plenty of rivals. Ring, the third baseman, batted .367. Watson, the right fielder, hit .333. Tosheff compiled a 6-1 record.

"It was a pretty good group," Andres said.

Andres had a magic touch that season. Twenty-eight times he called for a pinch hitter. Fourteen times the pinch hitters reached base.

The Hoosiers won their first seven games and nine of their first 10. They won seven of their last eight games, including an 8-5 win over Purdue that clinched their first conference crown since 1938.

This was the second year of NCAA tourney competition and Indiana was invited to the District 4 playoffs, set for Western Michigan and Kalamazoo, Michigan. Purdue and Notre Dame also received invitations along with the host Broncos.

"It wasn't as big a deal as it is now," Andres said. "Usually they picked teams that won their leagues."

IU faced Western Michigan on a non-conference roll. The Hoosiers had won 13 straight against non-Big Ten competition. Their last loss had come against Notre Dame on May 1 of the previous year. But shoddy defense did them in.

At least the trip wasn't expensive. The total cost was $230.05. That included $11.50 for the team to see a movie. There is no record of what the team saw, although the major pictures that year were "All The King's Men" and "Twelve O'Clock High."

NCAA Near Miss

For Jeff Calcaterra, it was two at-bats in one game against a future major league reliever. One ended with a home run, the other a strikeout. That neither produced a victory was beside the point in IU's 1996 return to NCAA relevance.

"It was a fun experience knowing that we could compete at that level," said Calcaterra, an assistant coach on that team.

The Hoosiers hadn't had this kind of fun since 1949, the only other time they had qualified for NCAA action. That one-and-done trip was ancient history for a '96 squad looking to make a postseason run in Wichita, Kansas.

First up, top-ranked Wichita State.

"I thought we got hosed on our seed," coach Bob Morgan said. "We got Wichita State because we were a sixth seed and we shouldn't have been seeded that low."

Opening with Wichita State was bad. Opening in the Shockers' home park was worse.

"They draw 9,000 to 10,000 a game there," Morgan said. "They try to intimidate you there—the team and their fans. I knew it would be a tough environment, but I knew we were capable."

Capabilities included a 16-1 streak entering NCAA regional action. Still, the Hoosiers didn't know how they'd react.

"It was a new experience for us," Calcaterra said. "Wichita was 50-6 and ranked No. 1. We were playing at their place in front of their fans. They had a turf infield and a grass outfield. It was a 7 o'clock game, under the lights."

The scouting report said pitch Wichita State away, but when Hoosier pitching ace Dan Ferrell did, he was rocked by a series of opposite field hits.

"They kept rifling balls down the right field line and went ahead 4-0 after two innings," Calcaterra said. "So we changed strategy and started throwing them inside. They didn't score again."

Indiana didn't score at all. Its only chance ended when a Wichita State outfielder climbed the fence to rob Steve Smella of a three-run home run. In came reliever Brandon Looper—who later pitched for the St. Louis Cardinals—and out went Hoosier comeback hopes.

"We were a good fastball hitting team and he was a fastball guy," Morgan said. "We hit the ball off him, but right at guys. "If Smella hadn't gotten robbed, if that kid hadn't made that play, we'd have had momentum. We'd have been very tough to beat."

IU edged Delaware 10-8 in the loser's bracket for the first NCAA tourney victory in school history. That set up a game with Rice, which had a pair of future major leaguers in Lance Berkman and Matt Anderson. The stakes were high—the loser went home, the winner advanced.

The back-and-forth game was tied at 7 entering the eighth inning when Anderson entered the game. Rice's relief ace had a 100-mph fastball and an intimidating reputation. His first batter was Mike Crotty, who would finish as one of the top home run hitters in Indiana history.

"Anderson's first warm-up pitch goes to the backstop," Calcaterra said. "It was a psyche-job kind of thing. But it didn't bother Mike. He was kind of a country boy from Ohio. He looked like he had a 50-year-old body. He had a bad back. He was bowlegged. But he had great wrists and power. He could get around on guys with velocity."

Anderson had velocity. The future Detroit Tiger relief pitcher's warm-up pitches popped into the catcher's mitt like small explosions.

"Anderson is gassing it up and the place is oohing and ahhing," Calcaterra said. "Mike isn't phased by it. He just stands there watching. And then the first pitch, I don't know how fast it was, but Mike put it off the scoreboard."

"He hit that thing a country mile," Morgan added.

With IU leading 8-7 in the bottom of the eighth, Rice had two men on with two out. Hoosier pitcher Ryan Graft got two strikes on Berkman, later an All-Star outfielder with the Houston Astros. The third strike never came. Berkman ripped what would become the game-winning hit.

"I'll never forget that," Morgan said. "Berkman fouls off seven pitches before he finally hits the shot to give them the lead."

IU had one last chance in the ninth. With two out and Rice ahead 11-8, Smella faced Anderson. He had more power than Crotty, but Anderson didn't care. He went power to power and neither player blinked.

"Smella fouled off like 21 pitches," Calcaterra said. "There were sliders and fastballs. The guy was throwing hard, like 90-mph sliders. Smella stayed right with him. He was a fighter. A scrappy guy. He finally struck out, but that didn't matter to me. It was one of the greatest at bats I've seen. His determination was phenomenal."

But it wasn't enough.

"If we had won that game," Morgan said, "we'd have been in the regional semifinals against Cal-State Fullerton. I'd like to have seen our chances if we had made it."

Tourney Title

Indiana was going nowhere fast in late April of '96. It was fifth in the Big Ten standings with a 10-8 record. Given only the top four teams made the league tournament, the pressure was on.

The Hoosiers responded with the best stretch run in school history. They won 15 in a row, including eight straight against Big Ten teams, to clinch a spot in the league tournament at Penn State, then won three of four games there to win an automatic bid.

"We swept Michigan State and then we swept Purdue," Calcaterra said. "We got hot at the right time."

IU went from fifth to second, finishing a half-game behind Penn State (19-8). It was led by catcher Matt Braughler, who won the Big Ten batting crown with a .444 average, and base stealing threats Ryan Dillion (36 steals) and Brian Harris (who had a school-record 50 steals in 1997). Ferrell, Brian Partenheimer and Ryan Graft led a solid pitching staff.

"We had a good combination," Morgan said. "We had good hitting. We pitched well. We played good defense. The team chemistry was very good. We had talented players and they all had good years for us. Everything fell into place."

The Hoosiers beat Illinois and its ace, Brett Weber, 6-3 in the tourney opener, then took out Penn State 6-2 to reach the finals. Illinois advanced out of the loser's bracket and ended IU's win streak with an 8-5 victory, setting up a one-game finale.

The Illini started Weber again. He had led the league in ERA (1.84) and victories (6). The Hoosiers countered with Graft, their No. 3 pitcher, with Ferrell set for relief. Indiana came out swinging. IU pounded out 16 hits, committed no errors and made crucial pitches.

"Ryan threw the best game of his career," Calcaterra said.

When he got in trouble in the eighth, Ferrell came in and got a double play to end the inning, then struck out the side in the ninth.

The Hoosiers were headed to Wichita.

Everett Dean was making his Indiana baseball coaching debut in 1925 with a spring southern trip. The Hoosiers were set to board the train to begin would be the most successful season in school history. They won their final six Big Ten games to claim their first ever conference championship with a 9-2 record. It was the first of three league crowns under Dean (also 1932 and '38) and four overall (1949). That doesn't include IU's 1996 Big Ten tourney title.

No one knew what to expect in the spring of 1949. Coach Donald Danielson, a former IU player, had left after one interim year—the 1948 season—in which the Hoosiers went 15-10, but just 3-9 in the conference. Coach Ernie Andres took over and made an instant impact. Indiana won its first seven games and nine of its first 10. It won the Big Ten title with an 8-4 record and earned an NCAA tourney bid. It lost 8-3 to Western Michigan and finished with an 18-5 record.

Jim McGee (left) and Bill Tosheff were the Hoosiers' dominant pitchers in 1949. McGee got a huge 8-5 victory against Purdue to clinch a share of the league title. Tosheff was 7-0 before losing to Purdue 7-1 in the second game of the double header. He lasted just over an inning.

Don Ritter saved his best for last. The senior first baseman blossomed into the Hoosiers' first first-team All-American in 1949. He hit .392, including .439 in Big Ten play. He also was 2-0 as a relief pitcher. He could also play defense with just four errors in 191 chances for a .979 fielding percentage.

Don Colnitis was the starting pitcher against Western Michigan in the 1949 NCAA opening round. He was rocked for four hits in the second inning. Add three Hoosier errors and the Broncos scored six runs in the inning, too big a deficit for IU to overcome. The 8-3 loss ended Indiana's first NCAA appearance. The next wouldn't come until 1996.

Ernie Andres was a rookie head coach in 1949. He had earned his fame as a player, first with the Hoosiers in the late 1930s, then with the minor league Louisville team of the American Association, later with the Great Lakes Naval Training Team during World War II, finally with the Boston Red Sox and two other American Association squads. What he lacked in coaching experience he made up for in results. IU won its first conference crown since 1938.

Bill Stearman was a two-sport athlete for the Hoosiers in the late 1940s. He played basketball and baseball. As a baseball player, he had a career batting average of .209 with three triples and 10 runs batted in. He is best known as one of the most successful high school basketball coaches in Indiana history. He won 714 games to rank third all-time behind Jack Butcher (806) and Howard Sharpe (724).

The Hoosiers' 6-4 victory over Illinois in the title game of the 1996 Big Ten tournament set off a boisterous celebration. IU had come in as the second seed behind Penn State. Still, the Hoosiers were the hottest team with eight straight league victories. They beat Illinois and Penn State to open tourney action, then lost to Illinois 8-5 in the double-elimination event to set up their victorious finale.

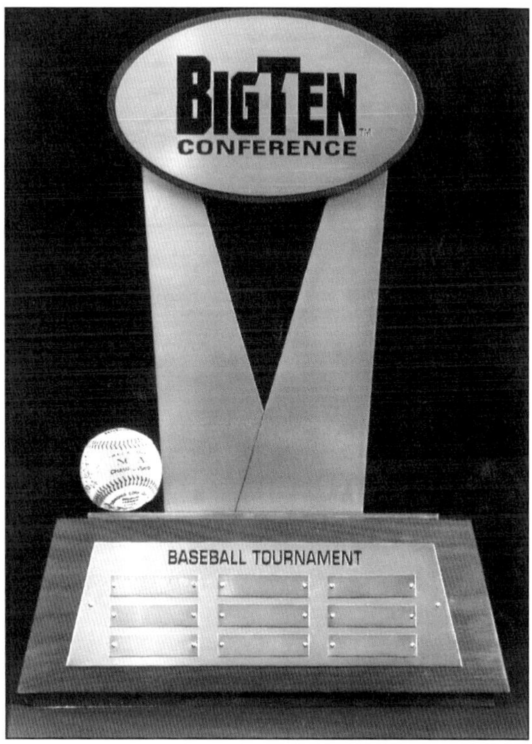

Indiana played in five Big Ten Tournaments before 2004 and won one—in 1996. That year the Hoosiers won their final eight conference games, swept series from Michigan State and Purdue, and finished second behind Penn State. Their hot streak continued with tourney victories over Illinois and Penn State to reach the finals. They beat the Illini to advance to NCAA action for the second time in school history (the first came in 1949). IU's other league tourney berths came in 1991, 1993, 2002, and 2003.

The Hoosiers came into the 1996 Big Ten tourney with a 1-4 record in their previous two league events. They posted a 3-1 record to win the championship and earn their first NCAA tourney bid since 1949.

Pitcher Dan Ferrell won nine games during IU's NCAA qualifying 1996 season. He set a school record by pitching 105.2 innings. He also started a record 16 games and completed what was then a record-tying eight of them. His 104 strikeouts are the third most in school history, behind Vernon Wilshere's 109 in 1934 and Claron Veller's 107 in 1931. Ferrell finished his career with a 17-16 record and a 4.50 ERA.

Bob Morgan arrived at IU in 1984 with a reputation for producing winners. In stops at Wooster and Kent State, he had never had a losing season and won at least 40 games three times in eight years. His first four Hoosier teams won at least 43 games, but couldn't crack the Big Ten's upper echelon. That changed in 1996, when Indiana finished second to Penn State in the regular season, then won the tourney and the automatic NCAA bid.

Third baseman Mike Crotty made the 1996 Big Ten all-tourney team as well as making academic all-conference. The last home run of his career came against Rice's Matt Anderson in the '96 NCAA tourney. Anderson went on to become a relief pitcher with the Detroit Tigers.

Although known more for his power and run production, Mike Crotty (diving back to first) had enough speed to draw pitchers' attention. He stole 11 bases in his career. But it was his slugging ability that helped IU to a second-place finish in the Big Ten and the conference tourney championship in 1996. During that season he led the team in hits (95), doubles (16, tied with Kyle Kramer), home runs (10, tied with Steve Smella), runs batted in (64) and slugging percentage (.573).

Brian Harris was coming into his own as a base stealer in 1996. He had 17 that year to finish behind Ryan Dillion (36) on the team. The next season Harris would set a school record with 50 steals.

Three

A Thousand Victories

Snow flew, wind blew, and the Hoosiers knew.

Forget Bob Morgan's Gatorade and ice water bath. March in Champaign had morphed into January. It snowed hard enough to delay IU's 2003 Big Ten opener at Illinois by 30 minutes. It was perfect weather for skis, not for bats.

"It was freezing," Calcaterra said, "but we had to play."

Nobody expected IU to arrive with Morgan still a victory shy of 1,000. The Hoosiers had hosted Wright State (5-12) three days earlier and everyone figured the milestone would happen then.

"There was a lot of anticipation," Calcaterra said. "There were a lot of people, like staff members, not usually there. Coach was kind of quiet. He told the team to play good baseball and not concentrate on 1,000."

The players couldn't help themselves. They planned a post-victory celebration.

"We thought it would be a big deal happening at home," pitcher Ryan Smith said. "We talked about dumping ice water and Gatorade on Coach. We joked about it. We would have been happy to have it happen here. . . . But it didn't."

Wright State didn't let it, rallying for a 7-6 victory with three runs in the eighth inning that spoiled everything. With Big Ten play set to start, Morgan went with his younger pitchers and they couldn't hold the lead.

"We wanted to do it at home for him," all-Big Ten second baseman Corby Heckman said. "His family was in town; his mother was here, a lot of people who played for him, a lot of friends. Unfortunately, it didn't happen."

And so it was on to Champaign. Pitcher Jacob Carey shut down the Illini on five hits while right fielder Kevin Mahar, designated hitter Nick Evans, shortstop Seth Bynum, and Heckman drove in runs in the 4-0 victory.

"Jacob Cary did a great job pitching for us," Morgan said. "He set the tone. Even though the elements were tough with the snow and how cold it was, he pitched an outstanding game and we got some very timely hits."

Morgan couldn't enjoy the moment long. The Hoosiers came right back to play the second game of the doubleheader and lost 9-2. Still, he had reached a milestone only 25 other coaches in baseball history had achieved.

"Coach had a big smile and normally you don't see that out of him," Calcaterra said. "He's pretty stern and pretty firm-faced all the time. But he was happy about the way we swung the bats, played good defense and pitched well."

And if it came three days later than expected, it still came. "He still got it," Smith said. "It was good to be here when Coach won." And what about that water-and-Gatorade moment? "We never got to do it," Smith said. "It was too cold. Not a nice baseball environment."

Morgan didn't care. "You've got to be fortunate to win that many games," he said. "It's a nice milestone, but all that does is speak volumes for the players who have played for me and the coaches who have coached under me and the managers and trainers. They've all been part of that. It hasn't been just the Bob Morgan show. When I reflect that only 25 other people in the history of the game have done it, it takes your breath away. It puts you in some pretty elite company."

Coach Bob Morgan received a plaque from athletic director Terry Clapacs commemorating his 1,000th career victory on April 2, 2003. Entering the 2004 season, Morgan averaged 37 victories over his 28-year coaching career. That included 20 years at Indiana.

True freshman pitcher Troy Ragle got the call when coach Bob Morgan decided not to put personal accomplishment over team priority. So what that Morgan's 1,000th career victory was at stake? With IU set to face struggling Wright State in late March of 2003, with Big Ten action looming in a few days, Morgan wanted to save his veteran pitchers. He would go with youth on the mound and, for four innings, it worked. Ragle held Wright State to one run as the Hoosiers took a 3-1 lead. Then Wright came out, three other inexperienced pitchers faltered and, in the end, so did Indiana. Center fielder Brad DeStefano's two hits, including a double, and two stolen bases weren't enough. Neither was second baseman Corby Heckman's one-out double in the bottom of the ninth. When third baseman Vasili Spanos, the eventual Big Ten batting champ, and pinch hitter Kenny Marrs struck out swinging, IU had lost 7-6. The milestone would have to wait.

In 28 years as a coach, Bob Morgan has had just one losing season. His 1985 IU team set the school record with 57 victories. Four other teams have won more than 40 games. The culmination came on March 26, 2003, when Morgan won his 1,000th career game. It was his 712th win at Indiana. Morgan was the 12th active coach and 26th overall to surpass 1,000 victories. His record after the 2003 season was 1,019-525-6.

Entering the 2003 season, Bob Morgan ranked 12th among active college coaches in victories. Here is the list: 1. Augie Garrido, Texas (1,380-666-8). 2. Gene Stephenson, Wichita State (1,357-422-3). 3. Chuck Hartman, Virginia Tech (1,338-705-8). 4. Larry Hayes, Texas Tech (1,320-739-2). 5. Larry Cochell, Oklahoma (1,246-712-3). 6. Mike Martin, Florida State (1,239-163). 7. Richard Jones, Illinois (1,160-670-5). 8. Ron Polk, Mississippi State (1,157-558-1). 9. Gary Adams, UCLA (1,109-832-12). 10. Mark Marquess, Stanford (1,093-533-5). 11. Jay Bergman, Central Florida (1,013-562-3). 12. Bob Morgan, Indiana (985-504-6).

Jeff Calcaterra (center) has been around for a majority of Bob Morgan's victories as a player and an assistant coach. Calcaterra was the team captain as a senior in 1992. His best year came in 1991 when he hit .322 with 10 doubles and 25 RBIs. A catcher, he threw out 27 consecutive runners his senior year to earn all-Big Ten honors.

Senior right hander Jacob Cary carried Hoosier hopes for a successful Big Ten beginning as well as coach Bob Morgan's 1,000th victory in late March of 2003. He rose to that challenge, overcoming Illinois hitters and sub-30-degree wind chill to throw a five-hit shutout in IU's 4-0 victory.

Coach Bob Morgan's 1,000th victory was still in doubt until right fielder Kevin Mahar drove in what proved to be the winning run with a sixth-inning single against Illinois. He was one of four Hoosiers to drive in runs in the 4-0 victory as IU achieved two goals—getting Morgan to 1,000 wins and winning the opening game of a Big Ten series, something that didn't happen at all the previous season.

Indiana has played baseball since 1896, winning nearly 1,800 games in that span. The Hoosiers won 350 games in the 1990s under Bob Morgan. All the home games were at Sembower Field, the site of all IU home contests since 1951. Morgan is pushing for a new stadium that he said would help IU become a factor on the national scene.

FOUR

Early Days, Early Struggles

The early Hoosiers didn't have Mighty Casey to terrorize pitchers, but they did have, in 1870, John Rice. Records from those years are sparse, but the 1894 Arbutus (IU's yearbook) listed as a tradition that, "in 1870, left-hander John Rice knocked a very live ball from home plate clear across Second Street."

Second Street was in play because Indiana played at University Athletic Field, which was located in what is now Seminary Square, in the block surrounded by Walnut, College, First, and Second streets. Home plate was near the intersection of Walnut and First streets.

Seminary Square also was the site of the university until 1885, when a fire caused the school to move the campus to near where the Sample Gates are now.

On the mound there was a pitcher called Pritchard whom the 1894 Arbutus described as being, in 1884, "the first master of the curve in the university." The 1893 yearbook described the exploits of pitcher Fred Cornell, who in 1886 "struck out at least 15 in every game."

IU baseball took on an organized appearance in 1867 with the formation of the University Baseball Club. Still, the game was nothing like it is today. There were no regulation bats, no gloves, no catchers' masks or pads or shields. The pitching rubber was 55 feet from home plate (now it's 60-foot-6) and until 1887 pitchers threw under-handed. Batters often got four strikes (foul balls didn't count) and five balls.

One of the more eccentric players in the late 1860s was catcher Edwin C. McIntire. He caught without a glove or a mask or any protective padding. He did wear high-topped boots, which he took off while batting. He ran the bases in socks.

Not many were around to see him. The student body was 100. There were eight professors.

By 1883, IU began competing against colleges on a regular basis (losing its first game that year to Asbury College, now DePauw, by a 23-6 score), although official records weren't kept for another 13 years. Part of that was due to the blurring of amateur and professional players. The NCAA didn't exist then and the rules that were on the books weren't always followed.

In 1890 Indiana won the state championship, although the means produced controversy. The 1893 Arbutus described it as being "badly tainted with professionalism." The consequences were felt in 1891, The Arbutus reported, when "baseball was under a cloud. There was no interest and players were few."

That was an era of "tramp athletes" and "ringers," when many athletes were not enrolled at the universities they played for and could play as many years as they wanted.

Everything was resolved by 1895, when IU rolled to an 11-1 record. However, it did lose an exhibition game to the faculty that year, 8-7. Pitching for the faculty was C.J. Sembower, the starting shortstop in 1893 and a senior reserve in 1894. He would go on to become a longtime Hoosier professor and athletic department representative. Sembower Field would be named for him.

Indiana's official baseball debut occurred in 1896 and it was a smashing success. The Hoosiers rocked Butler's baseball world with a 45-4 victory on April 11 of that season. Later they edged Michigan 11-10 in a disputed score, although the reason for the dispute is uncertain. They finished with a 6-3 record. In fact, they had five straight winning seasons before a new century brought inconsistency.

In 1898 they moved into Jordan Field, located in what is now a parking lot just east of the Memorial Union. Until 1925, Jordan Field was also used for football and track. It had no outfield fences, although right field was later separated from Seventh Street by a row of hedges. The nearby Jordan River was prone to spring flooding, which ruined many early season practices and games. The facility was named for David Starr Jordan, university president from 1885 to 1891.

Indiana joined what is now the Big Ten in 1899, but it didn't officially compete in baseball in the conference until 1906. It wasn't an auspicious debut season—the Hoosiers went just 1-5 in league play. The victory came against Purdue, 3-1. Back then the Big Ten was called the Western Conference (sometimes referred to as the Big Nine). With the addition of Ohio State in 1912, the conference became the Big Ten.

Life wasn't easy for the early Hoosiers. They often struggled to find games, and then struggled to win them. They played high school teams, club teams and little known college teams. Two of their seven victories in 1902 came against Indianapolis Shortridge High School by a combined score of 38-5. Three years later, they beat Bloomington High School 6-3.

Baseball got a big supporter when William Lowe Bryan became university president on January 21, 1903. The former Hoosiers second baseman—he played as a senior in 1884—served as president for 35 years, the longest tenure in IU history. He is the only Indiana letterman to be named president.

There was no official coach for the first three seasons, then 15 coaches in the next 25 years. Nobody lasted more than three years.

One highlight occurred in 1908 when Morris "Johnny" Johnson threw the first no-hitter in school history when he beat Northwestern, 1-0. The lone run came on team captain Clarence Cartwright's inside the park home run.

The next highlight came in 1913 under the direction of coach Arthur Berndt, a former Hoosier player. He led Indiana to second place in the Big Ten with a 6-3 record. But victories decreased, the coaching carrousel continued and the Hoosiers returned to being a conference after-thought.

IU did land one of the most famous assistant coaches in the country when Hall of Fame Chicago Cubs pitcher Mordecai "Three-Fingers" Brown became the pitching coach in 1920. Brown won at least 20 games six straight years for the Cubs in the early part of the century with a career earned run average of 2.06. However, the Hoosiers went just 7-7 in his only season. They did win their final four games, including a sweep of Purdue.

With financial support from Waseda University of Tokyo, Indiana embarked on the longest road trip in school history in 1922 when it went to Japan over spring break. Waseda officials offered to pay for the trip—they'd done the same thing for the University of Washington in previous years—and IU coach George Lewis jumped at the chance. The 1923 Arbutus reported that 60 players tried out for the trip and Lewis selected 12.

Those 12, plus coaches and three other students, including senior team manager Ernest Pyle, who would go on to journalistic stardom as a correspondent in World War II, endured a storm-tossed boat ride that left everyone seasick. The Hoosiers recovered and went 2-7-1 in the month-long trip that used up the bulk of its season. It played only three official games, going 1-2 against Purdue.

Lewis resigned as coach in 1923 to take a job with Showers Brothers Furniture Company in Bloomington. Basketball coach Leslie Mann was set to take over. He even started teaching a new course, Fundamentals of the Game, in which he showed more than 400 slides that demonstrated how to play baseball.

But Mann never got the chance to put his demonstration into use. Roscoe "Cow" Minton, a former Hoosier catcher and football halfback, became the coach, with little success. IU was 11-23-1 in his two seasons.

It was time for a change. Enter Everett Dean.

Zora Clevenger (second row, far left) was one of the giants of the early IU sports era. He played shortstop and in 1902 showed a flair for the dramatic. With the Hoosiers playing Minnesota and trailing 10-8 with two on and two out in the bottom of the ninth, he hit a three-run home run for the victory. Clevenger went on to coach the Hoosiers for two seasons—compiling a 16-23-1 record in 1905 and '06—before becoming IU's long-time athletic director. He is pictured with the 1901 Hoosiers.

Right hander Lee Streaker took the mound—or what little there was of it—in this 1894 photo at University Athletic Field. The field, also known as Seminary Field, was located where Seminary Park is now just south of the downtown square in Bloomington. It was used until 1898, when Jordan Field was built.

Jordan Field was the home of IU baseball from 1898 to 1951. It was located just to the east of what is now the Memorial Union. The field also was used for football games and track meets until 1925. ROTC training parades also were conducted there. This view is looking from the north atop the HPER Building.

Official records weren't kept before 1896 season, so the exploits of these 1894 Hoosiers are hazy. The 1894 Arbutus reported their record as 6-2. The team consisted of pitcher Cliff Utter (also the team captain), catcher Frank Ferguson, shortstop Frank Dailey, first baseman C.W. McMullen, second baseman Harry Scholler, third baseman H.W. McDowell, left fielder Claude Malott, center fielder-pitcher Lee Streaker and right fielder Ed Harris. The manager was Harry Axtell. The coaches were Berryhill and McIntyre (no first names listed). The reserves included C.J. Sembower, whose long tenure with the university as an English professor and faculty committee member for the university's athletic association resulted in IU naming its baseball field after him.

The 1904 Hoosiers produced the first outstanding record of the official era. They went 11-5 to set a school record for victories that wasn't broken until the 1919 squad went 13-9-1. Pictured, from left to right: (front row) shortstop Zora Clevenger, third baseman Harry Bradbury, catcher Daniel McIntosh, right fielder John O'Donnel, center fielder Frank Hare, left fielder Jasper Ross, and Albert Penn; (back row) team manager Long, pitcher Patrick Boyle, pitcher Morton Hunter, pitcher Don River, pitcher Mike Way, first baseman Homer Aikman, and second baseman Edward Boyle.

The Hoosiers were playing for nothing but pride in this June 9, 1924, game with Purdue at Jordan Field. Nearly 3,000 fans watched as this unidentified IU hitter joined with teammates for a 6-5 season-ending victory. It gave the Hoosiers an 8-12-1 record, 4-5 in the Big Ten. It was the last game for coach Roscoe Minton. The next year, the Everett Dean era began.

Sherman Minton's IU athletic exploits (a standout hitter and outfielder in baseball, a halfback in football) from 1911 to 14 were overshadowed by his post-college accomplishments. He served as an infantry captain in France during World War I. He was later a U.S. Senator and a justice in the U.S. Supreme Court. He retired from the Supreme Court in 1956 and died in 1965 at age 74.

Paul Parker was a baseball and basketball standout for the Hoosiers in the early 1920s. He was described in a cutline from that era as, "A sensational basketball center, ranges around first base. He is lanky and gets them whether wide or high."

Walter Wichterman was a sweet-swinging outfielder and team captain for the Hoosiers under coach Roscoe Minton in the early 1920s. The Hoosiers didn't have much success in Minton's two seasons, going 11-23-1.

FIVE

Resurrection Under Everett Dean

Everett Dean could practice what he preached. A standout Hoosier basketball and baseball player from 1919 to 1921, he got a contract offer from Hall of Fame manager Connie Mack of the Philadelphia Athletics. But Mack rescinded the offer when Dean expressed concern about baseball's reputation in the aftermath of the 1919 Black Sox scandal (members of the Chicago White Sox were accused of trying to throw the World Series). Instead, Dean became a successful basketball and baseball coach at Carleton College in Northfield, Minnesota.

In 1924, at age 26, Dean returned to his alma mater to coach both sports. IU had an enrollment of 3,000. There were no scholarships or recruiting services. You found players through high school coaches and alumni contacts.

Dean thrived.

"Everett Dean was a good Christian," said Bob Dro, a standout Hoosier player in the late 1930s. "More so than any person I've seen in the athletic business. And he knew his baseball and basketball."

The results were immediate. The Hoosiers won their first Big Ten title in his first season. They were 9-2 in the Big Ten in 1925, highlighted by a three-game sweep of Purdue.

Dean endured losing records the next two seasons—IU went 6-9 and 7-13. He never had another one.

"Everett was pretty intense, but also pretty straight laced," said Ernie Andres, who played baseball and basketball for Dean. "He was precise, kind of take your time. You go here and there. He was that way in both sports. He went through everything very carefully. He tried to instruct you as far as the right way to do things, and to do it all the time."

Still, Dean understood players had lives beyond the ball field. Consider these excerpts from a team manager to the IU student newspaper concerning the 1925 spring trip:

"Left Macon 10:30 Saturday night. Train ahead of ours wrecked with resulting seven-hour delay. Ward Belmont girls returning from vacation furnished company for all 32 hours. Team all in."

Or this:

"[Catcher Earl 'Red'] Moomaw stole home in the eighth inning, evidently thinking of his girl from Bluffton [Indiana], who is to meet him at the train upon his arrival home."

Dean's power of persuasion stretched well beyond state borders. Danny Danielson, a standout multi-sport athlete from North Dakota, was convinced by Dean's pitch. It was sweetened by a job that would pay for room and board. Danielson worked at the Graham Hotel in Bloomington, later at the Sigma Chi house, before graduating in 1942.

"In those days," Danielson said, "tuition was like $35 a semester, and $10 of that was for out of state."

SECOND TITLE

The Hoosiers had middle of the pact conference teams until 1932, when they won the championship with a 6-2 record, 13-2 overall by overcoming a series of injuries.

First, ace pitcher Ralph Gatti had his tonsils removed just before the start of the season. After winning his first four decisions, he was sidelined for a month when he fractured his right wrist while performing on the rings in gymnastics class.

Gatti returned in time for a Big Ten showdown with Purdue. With the league title on the line, he allowed just two earned runs in an 8-3 victory.

Another pitcher, Claddie Bailey, was hit with a line drive just above his eye and needed stitches. Third baseman Johnny Banka suffered lacerations to his left arm and leg after overturning his car to avoid a dog.

Even Jordan Field took a hit when a windstorm destroyed the deteriorating backstop that had been in place since 1900. A new backstop of wood and wire screen was installed.

With Gatti finishing 5-0, fellow pitcher Clifton Wright going 6-2 and outfielder Stanley Saluski batting a team-leading .429, IU won the Big Ten title. It was the university's fourth league crown that season following championships in cross country, wrestling, and indoor track.

But the Hoosiers endured criticism over the baseball title because they had played just eight games against three teams. The financial hardships caused by the Great Depression resulted in Big Ten athletic directors and coaches voting to cancel spring trips and schedule only 18 total games. Three of IU's games were rained out.

SUDDEN GOODBYE

Indiana was second in 1934 and won a school-record 19 games. It again won 19 games in 1937 and repeated as Big Ten runner-ups before winning the 1938 crown.

One of the most dominant pitchers of the Dean era was Vernon Wilshere. He went 17-2 with 197 strikeouts in 159 innings in 1933 and '34. That included a career earned run average of 1.12, which remains the IU record.

Wilshere was one of the nation's top pitchers in 1934, when he went 9-1 with 109 strikeouts in 82 innings. In conference action he was 5-1 with 71 strikeouts in 53 innings. That included striking out 16 in a 5-2 victory over Purdue.

Wilshere was so impressive during a victory over Temple that Philadelphia owner-manager Connie Mack, who attended the game, offered him a major league contract. Wilshere skipped his final season to sign. He won 10 major league games before arm trouble ended his career in 1938. He later served as an officer at Iowa pre-flight school during World War II.

"He was a good pitcher," Dro said. "A fastball pitcher. He had a lot of records back then. He really had it."

Dro had been recruited by Dean to play basketball and baseball. A standout athlete from Berne in northern Indiana, Dro had first told Dean he would come to Indiana. A visit by Purdue basketball coach Ward Lambert changed his mind, and he wrote Dean a letter telling him so. Dean asked for one last shot and Dro agreed. He and his father met the coach in an Indianapolis hotel.

"He won me over and I left with him for Indiana," Dro said. "Boy am I glad I did."

Freshmen were ineligible then so Dro played freshman baseball and basketball. He was a versatile player who could play any position and nearly did.

"I played wherever they wanted to have me—the outfield, the infield, catcher," he said. "I didn't pitch, but I should have pitched because I had a fastball. I was a little bit wild with it, but I had a good one."

Dro was a spectator in 1938 as the Hoosiers won their third Big Ten championship with a 7-3 record, 14-7-1 overall. He couldn't wait for his chance under Dean the next season.

And then Dean delivered a bombshell—he was leaving for Stanford.

"I'd come to play for Everett Dean, and then my first year I could play varsity, I was without him," Dro said. "We all had to adjust."

There were bigger adjustments ahead, both for Hoosiers and the world.

IU has never had a coach to compare with Everett Dean. His success in baseball and basketball makes him unique in school history. In baseball his teams compiled a 171-92-8 record overall, 78-55 in the Big Ten. Only two other Hoosier coaches had winning conference records, and they coached only one year (Fredrick Beebe was 4-3 in 1916; Roy Whisman was 5-4 in 1917). Dean's teams won three Big Ten titles. In basketball he had a record of 162-93, 96-72 in the Big Ten. The Hoosiers also won three league crowns.

Everett Dean was a two-sport standout during his playing days. He played baseball from 1919 to 1921, doing well enough to receive a contract offer to play for the Philadelphia Athletics. As a basketball player he received All-America honors as well as the Big Ten medal of academic and athletic excellence.

Russ Paugh pitched in the late 1920s. He led the Hoosiers with four victories in 1927, more than half their victory total of seven.

Before he went on to coaching and administrative success at Indiana, Paul Harrell was a top hitter. In his debut season of 1927, he hit .418. That was a sign of things to come. He finished with a career .404 average, the highest in school history.

Paul Harrell, whose nickname was "Pooch," hit for a .397 average in 1928, which was a slump for him, but still led the Hoosiers. That helped IU rebound from consecutive losing seasons to a 10-5 record.

Pitcher Claron Veller set the school single-season record for innings pitched and strikeouts in Big Ten games during the 1931 season. He pitched in 64 innings and struck out 83 batters, a school record. That strikeout record has stood the test of time. No other Hoosier pitcher has struck out more than 45 Big Ten batters in a season.

Claron Veller was the last pitcher opposing hitters wanted to see on the mound. In 1931 he allowed just nine hits all season. He walked just nine, meaning only 18 batters earned their way to base against him.

Ralph Gatti had quite a year in 1932. He went 5-0 to help the Hoosiers win their second conference championship. He got the clinching 8-3 victory over Purdue, allowing just two earned runs in his first start in a month after fracturing his right wrist during a physical education class.

Clifton Wright joined with Ralph Gatti to give IU a dominating one-two pitching punch in 1932. He was 6-2 that season. He had gone 3-0 the year before to finish his career with a 9-2 record.

Tragedy hit the Indiana team near the end of the 1934 season when second baseman Kenneth Dugan was killed in a car accident in Indianapolis. The slick fielding Dugan was hitting .272 and had been named team captain. "He was one of the finest infielders ever to play on Jordan Field," coach Everett Dean said in the June 9, 1934, *Indiana Daily Student*. "His death is a great personal loss to me."

Pitcher Vernon "Whitey" Wilshere was a big reason why Indiana went 35-8-1 in 1933 and '34. He compiled a 17-2 record in that stretch, striking out 197 batters in 159 innings with a career earned run average of 1.12. That ERA is the best in school history. Second is Robert Marr, who had a 1.50 ERA while pitching in the early 1960s. Wilshere had a brief career with the Philadelphia Athletics before arm trouble forced his retirement in 1938.

As a junior in 1938, Ernie Andres played a major role in IU's league championship, the last under coach Everett Dean. He led the team in hitting (.385) and runs (23). He had one of the season's biggest hits, a twelfth inning, two-out double that drove in Bill Smith for the winning run in a 3-2 victory over Purdue that helped the Hoosiers to the title. It was the second longest game ever played at Jordan Field, topped only by a 1-0 16-inning win against Ohio State in 1916.

Bob Dro never got to play for Everett Dean, although he was recruited by him. Dro hit .283 in 1939 under first-year coach Paul Harrell. Dro also missed Dean in basketball, although he did get to play for coach Branch McCracken. He was a member of the 1940 national championship squad.

The 1937 Hoosiers were in the middle of a Big Ten title hunt when this batting practice photo was taken. They wound up second with an 8-2 league record, and then came back the next year to win it all. Pictured are Babe Hosler (hitting), Bill Heldt (catching) and Ernie Andres (on deck). Andres was an outstanding two-sport athlete who went on to coach IU for 24 seasons. Coaching highlights included the 1949 Big Ten title, the school's first NCAA tourney bid and more than 400 career victories.

Six

War Years Successes

College athletics couldn't escape World War II's impact. Budgets were cut and players were lost—some by enlistment, others by draft.

The Hoosiers were hit the hardest in 1943, when they played just five games, none in the Big Ten.

Still, Paul Harrell continued Dean's coaching success throughout the 1940s. The former sweet-swinging Hoosier hitter—his career batting average of .404 from 1927–29 remains the school record—became the second IU coach to win 100 games (101-65-2) and had just one losing record in his nine seasons.

However, Harrell's longest-lasting claim to fame, or infamy depending on your perspective, was being the driving force—as athletic director and later supervisor of athletic buildings grounds—behind the design of Assembly Hall and Memorial Stadium. The idea was to build facilities that would have most of the seats on the two sides to provide a better view. In that era, it was difficult to sell seats at the ends.

But Harrell's 1940s-era basketball plans clashed with late-20th Century sensibilities.

Harrell got his idea from a North Carolina livestock pavilion and passed it on to an Indianapolis architectural firm. The results were 52,354-seat Memorial Stadium, completed in 1960, and 17,300-seat Assembly Hall, finished in 1972.

In theory, it was a good idea and resulted in a functional football stadium and a visually stunning basketball arena that ranks among the nation's most famous. In practice, it produced a fan-unfriendly, view-challenged basketball environment. Towering sides elevated spectators to unsurpassed heights and unexpected consequences. Elderly fans were unhappy. Balcony stuck spectators were miserable.

And so it continues. IU officials have long-range plans to either build a new basketball arena or renovate Assembly Hall, but no definitive timetable.

Superior Speed

The Hoosiers' best Big Ten finish under Harrell was second in his first season of 1939. They were 16-4 overall and 7-3 in the conference.

Even before that season started, Harrell liked the team's prospects. He told the Indiana Daily Student on March 3, 1939 that, "If we ever get on base, boy we're going to steal, steal, steal, steal. We've got speed in fellows like [Tom] Gwin, [John] Corriden and [Bob] Dro. [Ernie] Andres is fast, too. Boy, we're going to use it."

It paid off. IU won its first eight games, and seven of its last eight. But a late home loss to Michigan cost it a second straight conference title.

"We should have won it that year," said Danny Danielson, the second baseman on that team. "We had some great players. But losing to Michigan cost us."

The Hoosiers traveled cheap in those years. During a two-day trip to Minnesota in 1945, Harrell's expense report included $15.88 for dinner for 20 people.

IU drew well in 1947. A crowd of 4,000 at Jordan Field watched a 4-0 season-opening victory over Indiana Central. That helped the Hoosiers to a 9-1 start. They lost two games to Notre Dame and never recovered, finishing 12-7 in Harrell's final season.

Harrell's baseball coaching run ended when IU football coach-athletic director Bo McMillen resigned to become the head coach of the NFL's Detroit Lions in December of 1947. Harrell took over as A.D. and was too busy to coach baseball. So he asked Danielson, who was working in the alumni office, to be the interim coach for the spring of 1948.

Danielson had been a good enough player to sign a $1,000 bonus in 1942 to play in the Brooklyn Dodgers organization. He was one of eight college players signed by Brooklyn that year. Bob Dro was another. So was Jackie Robinson, the future Hall of Famer who broke major league baseball's color barrier five years later.

But after one year of minor league ball and four years in the Navy, Danielson's athletic career was over. By the time of Harrell's offer, Danielson already had given the university notice that he was leaving in June of 1948 to join New Castle (Ind.) Products. Still, the coaching offer was too good to resist.

"I said I'd love to coach," Danielson said. "I was very excited. I knew we had a team that was capable. We had pitching and defense and guys who could hit."

What he didn't have was luck. First, standout shortstop Del Russell—also the starting quarterback—had to leave after the spring trip because new football coach Clyde Smith wanted him at spring practice. Then, standout center fielder-pitcher Don Ritter was lost in the first game back from the spring trip with a broken ankle.

Without their two best players, a 7-0 start faded to an 8-10 finish and a final 15-10 record.

"We could have won the Big Ten," Danielson said. "And there were only two seniors on that team. Almost everybody was back. I knew we could be even better. But I was the interim coach, so it didn't matter."

Danielson went on to a successful business career. At the age of 83 in the summer of 2003 he was still vice chairman of the board for City Securities Corp. out of Indianapolis. His long ties with the university included being a 21-year member of the board of trustees (11 as chairman) and a director of the IU Foundation.

But by the summer of 1948, Danielson was in New Castle and Harrell was focused on finding a permanent coach. Once again, school officials went for Cream 'n Crimson ties. This time, it would last for 24 seasons.

Kermit Wahl showed off his vertical leap from the infield of Jordan Field in the early 1940s. Wahl was a career .292 hitter for coach Paul Harrell. Behind him is The Fieldhouse, where IU once played its basketball games. It is now called the Wildemuth Intramural Center.

Don Dunker was a standout pitcher in the early 1940s. In 1941, he had an earned run average of 1.80, which ranks seventh in the school's single-season list for pitchers who have thrown at least 50 innings. Dunker finished with a career ERA of 1.58, which is the fourth-best mark in school history.

There wasn't much Don Ritter couldn't do as an athlete in the late 1940s. As a basketball player, he scored 560 points with a career 9.2 average. He was a standout hitter and pitcher in baseball. He had a career batting average of .382. As a pitcher, he had a career record of 6-2 with a 4.57 earned run average. He was IU's first baseball All-American.

Ted Kluszewski (back row, third from right) supplied the power for Indiana, which went 5-5-1 in the Big Ten, 12-8-2 overall in 1945. He had a team-leading 10 RBIs and 11 runs in 11 Big Ten games. He hit .409 in league play, which ranked fourth on the team. He hit .477 in non-conference games, and a team-leading .443 overall.

Coach Paul Harrell (left) got plenty of help from team captain Al Kralovansky in 1945. Harrell compiled a record of 101-65-2 from 1939–47. His Hoosiers finished second in the Big Ten in 1939. After retiring from coaching, Harrell went on to serve as athletic director and the university's facilities manager. Kralovansky ranked just behind Ted Kluszewski as a hitting star that season.

Bob Miller was a strong-fielding third baseman who got better with the bat as the season went on in 1945. He batted .357 in Big Ten games, but struggled in non-league games with a .182 average. He led the team with 61 assists.

Al Kralovansky dominated non-conference pitching, hitting a robust .477 for the 1945 Hoosiers. Life was tougher in the Big Ten, where he struggled to hit .268. That gave him a season average of .368.

Freshman Mike Modak was the Hoosiers' best pitcher in 1945. He went 6-3 with 41 strikeouts in 60 innings. His strong start mirrored that of Indiana, which opened 9-0-1 and put itself in early contention for a conference title. But the Hoosiers won only three more games the rest of the season.

Bill Sarengach of East Chicago was IU's first returning World War II combat veteran to win a position on IU's athletic teams. The former infantry sergeant was wounded in action at Anzio and also at Cassino. He was a reserve third baseman. For the 1945 season he had only had one at bat, although he made the most of it with a hit.

Promising freshman righthander Willard Kopps had to leave IU on June 1 of the 1945 season to be inducted into the Army. He had gotten off to a solid start and was the winning pitcher over Purdue. He also lost to Northwestern. He finished with a 2-1 record. He was wild in league action with eight walks and one strikeout in nine innings.

Don Ritter hit a team-leading .382 with 29 hits and 45 total bases in 1946. It was his first year back after a brief stay with the Hoosiers in 1943 before joining the service for World War II. He was second on the team with 13 RBIs.

Harry Ritter (right) wasn't quite as explosive with the bat as his older brother Don. He hit just .083 in the 1946 season.

Another brother combination for the 1946 season was pitcher Ralph Brickner and catcher Art Brickner. Ralph fared well as a hitter, batting .308. Art had a .314 average. Ralph was 6-3 with a 2.32 ERA.

Third baseman Bill Stearman didn't make much of an impact in 1946, when he hit .143 and appeared in seven games. His best season came in 1948, when he hit .345.

He is officially listed as Donald Danielson in the IU record books. But he is better known as Danny Danielson, a former chairman of the IU board of trustees and IU Foundation director. Danielson was never on a losing team during his Cream 'n Crimson years. He was the second baseman from 1940 to 1942, with Indiana going 42-20 in that span. In his one year as interim head coach (1948), the Hoosiers were 15-10.

SEVEN

The Andres Era

You see images of Ernie Andres when he was young and strong and seemingly bulletproof, before age put the kryptonite into his superman athletic excellence. He played professionally in the American League and in the National Basketball League, the precursor to the NBA. He was the first IU and Big Ten player to score 30 points in a basketball game.

After his Hoosier run ended (24 years as a coach, 10 more in the alumni office), Andres moved to Bradenton, Florida. At age 85 in the summer of 2003, his mind remained sharp. Call it the benefits of a lifetime of working crossword puzzles. If he couldn't do all the physical things he once could, he could adjust.

"When I first moved down here, I had a ball," he said. "I played golf. I bowled. I used to have a lot of fun. Then my back went out on me and I had to give them both up.

Now I play bridge and read and work cross word puzzles. I watch TV. I do a little walking."

Don't challenge him to cross word puzzles.

"He was always very good at them," said Bob Lawrence, who played for and coached under Andres. "He'd take The New York Times puzzle and have that thing done in 10 minutes."

Andres' pro baseball playing career peaked in 1946 when, for 15 games, he was the Boston Red Sox's starting third baseman.

"After 15 games I was hitting .100 and you don't keep third baseman very long hitting .100," he said with a laugh.

Andres returned to the minors and was never called up again.

"I hit the top for about six weeks," he said. "It was the cup of coffee they talk about."

The cup wasn't lucrative.

"I can tell you exactly what I made," Andres said as if it was yesterday. "I signed one major league contract. I was a rookie, so it was probably the minimum, which is what it should have been. It was for $5,000."

Andres also played professionally for the NBL. He had a two-year stint for the Indianapolis Kautskies in the early 1940s, spent 52 months in the service during World War II, then another year as the Kautskies' player-manager.

"I got $35 a game, and $25 plus expenses on the road," he said.

Does he ever wonder what kind of money he could have commanded if he played today?

"Now-a-days I could have played one sport against the other. I'd have had a lot of fun."

TWO-SPORT STUD

Andres, a three-time all-Big Ten choice as a basketball player, made a big impact in baseball. One of the biggest helped the Hoosiers clinch the 1938 conference title. Facing a late-season showdown with Purdue, Andres had the game-winning double in the bottom of the 12th inning as Indiana won 3-2.

Not bad for someone whom Everett Dean didn't know could play the sport.

Andres attracted Dean's attention as a standout high school basketball player at Jeffersonville, Indiana. Actually, Dean was more interested in fellow Jeffersonville guard Bill Johnson, but took Andres because the two wanted to attend the same school.

"Everett never knew I could play baseball while he was recruiting me," he said. "He thought I could play basketball, but Johnson was the guy he was going after for basketball. Turns out I helped him more than Bill did."

That help came without a scholarship, which weren't offered in those years.

"They marked off my tuition and I got a job on the side," he said. "I'd spend two hours a night scrubbing the floors in The Fieldhouse for 35 cents an hour. That was my spending money. I also worked in the kitchen for my meals, and I lived with a family that didn't charge me anything."

Now, of course, players get their schooling paid for. They also are allowed off-season jobs.

"Schools give them everything, which is fine," Andres said. "I think they should. If a kid is giving it 100 percent in school and in the sport, he deserves it."

Ensuring that athletes gave 100 percent in the classroom during Andres' playing days was a role filled by physical education professor George Schlafer.

"He was tough," Andres said, "but fair. When I was a senior, I was the captain of the basketball team. I was taking a course from him. I had to come up with seven things for this course. I don't remember what they were, but I had only six.

"We were getting ready to play Xavier in Cincinnati and he wouldn't let me go until I got the seventh one done. The team left and I worked half the night and finally got it done. Then he let me go. I got there just in time for the game."

Schlafer was just as strict with Andres' basketball teammate, Paul Armstrong.

"He was taking some kind of dance class and was short a dance or two," Andres said. "So he had to go in a room with a Victrola (record player) and do his dances while the team was warming up. He got his dances in and got to play. But Schlafer wouldn't let him go until he did them."

While Andres had some good seasons as a player (he was a career .303 hitter), it was as a coach where he left his biggest mark. He was the first IU coach to win 400 games and 100 league contests. He finished with a 401-377-3 record (.513), 140-221-1 (.387) in the Big Ten.

"He was a good coach," Bob Lawrence said. "He was demanding, but he was kind of soft spoken and low key."

Still, Andres could find a higher key when necessary.

"I remember we were playing at Sembower Field and there was a storage room at the end of the dugout," Lawerence said. "Ernie came in upset about something that didn't go right for Indiana, so he kicks this bag of lime that was there. All the white lime came out and covered him. He looked like Casper the ghost."

The Hoosiers went 18-5 in Andres' first year, when they won the league championship, then didn't surpass that victory total until 1961, when they went 21-5-1 and finished third in the Big Ten. His 1964 team set a school record for victories (23) that lasted until the 1982 team won 25 games.

Recruiting was an early challenge because of the lack of scholarships.

"The first 10 to 12 years I coached, we had no scholarships," Andres said. "I could get them jobs. Maybe finagle in tuition, which wasn't much those days. Sometimes they just marked off tuition.

"Even at the end of my coaching, we only had five scholarships and you couldn't split them up. So you really had to be careful about who you offered."

Carefulness included honesty because back then, as now, the best players who didn't sign with major league teams usually went to southern schools, which offered year-round playing weather.

"If a kid had a scholarship to a good southern baseball school, I'd never tell him not to take it," Andres said. "There were several kids from the state of Indiana who had a chance to go south and they went south. You couldn't blame them. They got to play all year.

"What I emphasized was the academics. I thought as far as school, we had better than those southern schools had. I could talk to players about that."

Andres could also talk about the five no-hitters Hoosier pitchers threw under his direction.

The first came against Indianapolis on April 2, 1955, when Bernard Ratterman and Harold Summers combined for a nine-inning gem in a 9-1 IU victory. Ratterman allowed one run and one walk in five innings. Summers allowed nothing in four.

Ten days later, Bill Dooley and Summers combined on another no-hitter as the Hoosiers beat Bakalar Air Force Base 21-0. Dooley struck out eight and walked one in four innings. Summers struck out six and walked none in three.

Albin Hayes is the only Hoosier pitcher to lose a no-hitter. In seven innings he gave up two runs and six walks in a 2-1 loss to Ohio State on May 4, 1957.

Richard Scott was too much for the Louisville All Stars on April 13, 1963. He struck out seven and walked two in a 13-0 no-hit victory that lasted just five innings.

The final no-hitter during Andres' tenure came on April 17, 1971, when Jack Polance shut down Northern Illinois in five innings, 2-0. He struck out five and didn't walk a batter.

Perhaps the most colorful player to play under Andres was Bart Kaufman, who compiled a career .327 batting average in the early 1960s.

"Bart was baseball through and through," Andres said. "You could ask him any question about a major league player and he could give you the answer. When we rode the bus to games, guys would ask him all sorts of questions, like who led the league in hitting or who did this guy pitch for. He knew all the answers."

After three straight losing seasons near the end of his coaching run, Andres had one more success. The 1973 Hoosiers went 20-16, including a doubleheader sweep of Purdue. Andres retired as coach and moved into the alumni office.

"I really enjoyed it, working with all those young guys," Andres said. "Indiana has only been involved in a Big Ten (regular season) championship four times, and I coached on one and played on one. That's pretty satisfying."

And then it was time to leave the satisfaction for others.

Ernie Andres left a lasting impression on the Indiana program as a player and as a coach. He was a career .300 hitter as a player, and then became the first Hoosier coach to win 400 games and surpass 100 Big Ten victories. He coached from 1949 to 1973, giving him the longest run of any IU baseball coach. Also a basketball standout, Andres made first-team All-Big Ten in that sport in 1938 and '39. He earned All-American basketball honors in 1938. He played professionally in both sports.

Sam Esposito was a three-sport athlete at Indiana in the early 1950s, starring in football and basketball as well as baseball. Coach Ernie Andres, himself a two-sport Hoosier athlete (basketball and baseball), praised Esposito's athleticism and toughness. Esposito went on to become a utility player for the Chicago White Sox. He played on the 1959 White Sox team that reached the World Series. It lost to the Los Angeles Dodgers.

Although not a big hitter, Dennis Krueger could handle the bat in the mid-1960s. He had a career batting average of .255. He had five doubles, four triples and one home run among his 63 career hits.

Wayne Witmer had a solid career at IU in the mid-1960s. He was a career .250 hitter with five doubles, three triples and 23 runs batted in. The Hoosiers won a total of 60 games during his three seasons.

From 1966 to 1968, no Hoosier pitcher threw as well as Gary Sargent. He had a career earned run average of 1.57. He struck out 198 batters in 200 innings while walking only 78. Of the 62 runs scored on him, only 35 were earned. But he was hurt by a lack of run support, usually because he pitched against the best teams and best pitchers. As a result, he finished with a career record of 9-16.

Jim Cline went 1-0 with a 4.90 earned run average for the 1967 Hoosiers, who had a 14-23 record, 6-12 in the Big Ten.

Consistency made Gary Sargent one of the best pitchers in IU history. His 1967 ERA of 1.20 ranks second on the school's record books to Vernon Wilshere's 1.10 in 1934. Sargent had an ERA of 1.68 in 1968 and 1.97 in 1966. Those are three of the top-10 earned run averages ever posted for the Hoosiers.

Jack Campbell pitched on two of coach Ernie Andres' three 20-victory seasons. Campbell had a 2-1 record in those two years (1964 and '65), during which IU went 23-12 and 20-15. It was the only time in Andres' 24-year career he had consecutive 20-win seasons. Campbell also earned all-conference recognition as a hitter. He led IU in average (.361), runs batted in (28), triples (three), hits (43) and runs (31) in 1966.

Chuck Cline was a career .247 hitter for the Hoosiers during the late 1960s. He finished with five doubles, four home runs and 18 runs batted in.

Few pitchers were tougher to score on than Bill Gifford in 1968. He allowed just three runs all season, tying John Lobus for the team low. His 4-1 record tied Gary Sargent for the team high in victories. His 11 walks were the fewest allowed by any IU pitcher that year.

Pete Duhamel was a reserve player in the late 1960s. While he only had 111 career at-bats, he did show some power with four home runs.

Mike Baughman had a career batting average of .300 from 1968 to 1970. He led the Hoosiers in hitting in 1969 (.347) and '70 (.315). His best all-around year was in 1970 when he also led the team in hits (46), doubles (7), triples (3) and total bases (62).

Frank Grundler was a career .300 hitter for the Hoosiers in the early 1970s. He pounded out 16 doubles and nine home runs while driving in 64 runs. His best year was in 1971 when he led IU in slugging percentage (.462), total bases (82), runs batted in (34), home runs (6), doubles (6) and runs (24).

EIGHT

Decade in Transition

Why Miami? Why would a rookie head coach choose to open with the top-ranked Hurricanes, who had one of the nation's top programs?

"When I got the job," Bob Lawrence said, "I decided we had to go somewhere nice for a spring trip. I called Miami because I knew they had a nice field and had a top school."

Lawrence was young and aggressive then, not yet tempered by the hard realities Midwest schools faced against southern superpowers. He would face the best and the Hoosiers would be better for it, win or lose.

In time, however, Lawrence would recognize the price of such idealism.

"That was probably a mistake," he said. "They were ranked No. 1, were 18-2 and we hadn't been outside yet."

The mistake was quickly apparent to Lawrence, an Andres' assistant for the previous nine years. IU got off to a 1-6 start. Still, it wasn't all negative. The Hoosiers played Miami tough, losing 7-2, 4-2, and 7-6 in mid-March of 1974.

"We gave them some good games, so I was happy about that," Lawrence said.

The payoff came a month later when Indiana hosted Minnesota at Sembower Field. The Gophers were then, as now, a Big Ten power. The score was tied 8-8 going into the bottom of the seventh inning when IU catcher Ken St. Pierre belted a game-winning home run.

"There wasn't any doubt about that one," Lawrence said. "It almost ended up in the tennis courts beyond the left field fence."

That was the only time a Lawrence team beat Minnesota. The Gophers won the final 11 meetings.

"But that was one of the biggest wins we had," he said. "They were one of the better teams in the country that year."

Another big victory came against Pan American in 1976 as part of a spring trip to Texas. Pan American was a top-20 team for much of the 1970s and the Hoosiers played them frequently under Lawrence. IU split a four-game series in 1976, winning 11-7 and 1-0 and losing 7-6 and 8-0.

But perhaps the biggest memory of that trip for Lawrence came when he took his team across the border to Mexico. They did some sightseeing and shopping, and had lunch. They returned with Montezuma's revenge.

"Half the guys on the team got sick that night," Lawrence said. "We went to what was supposed to be a pretty good restaurant, but it didn't help. After that, I never took the team across the border for lunch again."

STANDOUTS

Lawrence said the best pitcher he ever coached was Gary Sargent. From 1966 to 1968, while Lawrence was an assistant coach, Sargent had a career earned run average of 1.57. He struck out 198 batters in 200 innings while walking just 78. However, he had a career record of 9-16.

"If I had to win a game," Lawrence said, "I'd have to go with Gary. He was the most consistent pitcher we ever had. He had a losing record because he always pitched the tough games against the tough teams. He'd lose like 2-1, 1-0."

Lawrence also mentioned Larry Rosin, who won 17 games from 1977 to 1979. That included a no-hitter on May 26, 1977, against Illinois. He struck out five and walked two in a 9-1 victory. Rosin ranks sixth in school history with 199 strikeouts.

"He had a very good career," Lawrence said.

While three Hoosiers won Big Ten batting titles during his years as coach—Jack Campbell in 1966, Barry Burnett in 1973 and Scott Weiner in 1976—Lawrence said his best hitter was Larry Blackwell, a lifetime .322 batter who never led IU in hitting.

"But he was a good clutch hitter," Lawrence said. "He got hits when we needed them. He was the best when it came to that."

Under Lawrence, IU annually ranked as one of the Big Ten's best hitting teams. The Hoosiers led the league in team average four times in his 15 years as an assistant and head coach. In 1976, they hit a robust .320.

The pitching was less consistent, a big reason why Lawrence had just one winning record in his seven years as head coach.

"We had pretty good hitting teams," he said, "but we never had the quality pitching that was needed. We had maybe one good pitcher a year, but not enough to go anywhere."

Lawrence's best year came in 1976. IU went 23-17 and finished third in the Big Ten with a 10-7 record. It led the league in hitting, topped by Scott Weiner's .453 mark. Outfielder Terry Jones led the conference in home runs (5), while he and Weiner shared the lead in RBIs (16 each). Pitcher John Barnfield led the team in victories (7) while Larry Rosen had the best ERA (3.55).

"It was a well-rounded team," Lawrence said. "Everybody worked well as a team that year."

If not for a seven-game league losing streak in mid-May, the Hoosiers might have made a title run. They won their final six conference games. That included sweeping a doubleheader from Purdue, 3-2 and 17-6. That was nothing new. Lawrence had a 10-4 record against the Boilermakers.

"Always beating them was big," he said. "We didn't have much trouble with them overall."

Trouble came against the rest of the Big Ten. Lawrence had losing records in his final four seasons and by 1981, he had moved on to become the supervisor for student teachers at the Health, Physical Education and Recreation building (HPER), a position he retained until retiring in the summer of 2002.

"I enjoyed by 15 years coaching at Indiana," he said. "It was a good experience. It was something I'll always remember. And when the time came, I was glad to get out and do something else."

Short Stay

Larry Smith replaced Lawrence as head coach in 1981. He had losing records his first two seasons, then guided IU to a school-record 26 victories (against 21 defeats) in 1983. That was the Hoosiers' first winning mark since 1976 and just their third since 1970.

They ended the 1983 season with a bang, winning six of their final seven games. The program was progressing, optimism was high and prospects were good.

Then Smith left and the search for a new coach began. It would result in the arrival of a coach with no Hoosier connection and deep Ohio roots, a man who had interviewed for the job three years earlier.

The program hasn't been the same since.

Bob Lawrence only played baseball one year at Indiana, but he made a lasting impression. He hit .472 to win the Big Ten batting title in 1958 and had an .849 slugging percentage, the second-best in school history. He was an assistant coach for nine years before taking over the program in 1974. His teams compiled a 132-164 record, including 44-71 in Big Ten play. His best conference finish was third in 1976.

Catcher Ken St. Pierre was an offensive and defensive force as a senior in 1974. Defensively he committed only two errors in 104 changes, a .981 fielding percentage. Despite the rigors of his position, he played in every game. He led the team in triples (7) and runs batted in (39). He was second in hitting (.313), doubles (11), runs scored (29) and hits (41). He was named first team All-American, only the second Hoosier to ever be so honored. The first was Don Ritter in 1949.

When Ken St. Pierre wasn't hitting baseballs, he was hitting would-be tacklers. Pierre (35) was a fullback on the football team in 1971 and '72.

Robin Cox was a steady hitter in the mid-1970s. He finished with a career batting average of .299 with 19 doubles, five triples and six home runs. He also drove in 55 runs.

Although recording more walks (156) than strikeouts (148), Dave Zuerner won 11 games and had a career earned run average of 5.27 from 1977 to 1980, mostly because it was so difficult to get a hit off him. He led the Hoosiers in fewest hits allowed in 1977 and '78. His best year came in 1977 when he recorded three complete-game shutouts and only allowed 24 runs all season. In 1979 he led the team with a 2.92 ERA.

When it came to hitting in the clutch, few hitters were better than Larry Blackwell. From 1979 to 1982, Blackwell consistently got the big hits to start rallies or drive in runs. He drove in 109 career runs with his 139 career hits. He also had power, slugging 19 home runs and 28 doubles.

Larry Rosin was a dominating pitcher in the late 1970s. He set a school record with eight complete games in 1977 that lasted until Chad Smith totaled nine in 1998. He compiled a 17-19 career record with a 5.03 ERA. His 199 strikeouts rank sixth in school history. He threw four shutouts. But his best game wasn't a shutout. On May 22, 1976, he no hit Illinois in a 9-1 victory. He struck out five and walked two. That was one of eight no-hitters thrown by an Indiana pitcher.

Other Hoosiers put up gaudier numbers than Larry Blackwell, who finished with a career batting average of .322. But he twice led IU in runs batted in, twice in home runs and twice in doubles. His .559 career slugging percentage ranks seventh in school history.

Larry Smith coached IU for just three seasons, from 1981 to 1983. His teams were 73-75-1 overall, 13-30-1 in the Big Ten. His last team was his best, winning 28 games and finishing third in the Big Ten.

Larry Blackwell, Jay Grochowski and Bob Waite (left to right) were co-captains on the 1982 team, which set a then IU record for victories, with 25. Grochowski led the team in at bats (175) that season. Blackwell led in total bases (90) and slugging percentage (.566). Waite led in stolen bases (27), walks (51) and runs (47). Waite's career .388 batting average ranks third in school history behind Paul Harrell (.404) and Alex Smith (.393).

Pitcher Mike Humphrey was IU's winningest pitcher in 1982 (6 wins) and 1985 (10). His 4.00 earned run average led the team in 1982 as did his eight complete games.

Mike Humphrey won 23 games from 1982 to 1985, which is tied for third on the school's all-time list. Only Brian Partenheimer (30) and Craig Williams (26) won more.

NINE

The Bob Morgan Turnaround

Smile lines have no business on Bob Morgan's face. His is the chiseled countenance of a man too focused for humor. You could see him at a poker table, the family car at stake, the hand shaky, flashing a glare that could shatter glass, daring you to show something better, looking as if he'd wring your neck if you did.

"There is an intimidation factor," said Jeff Calcaterra, assistant coach and former player. "As a player, there's some fear for the first couple of years. Then you get out of that and you just play."

Morgan coaches with steely-eyed intensity. He is demanding and tough. He makes points from mouthwash range.

"I tell guys, 'I'm not here to be your friend,'" he said. "Maybe once you graduate, we'll laugh and be friends and get a sandwich sometime. But now I'm here to be your dad away from home. I'm here to be your leader. I'm going to pat you. I'm going to kick you. I'm going to get on you."

You want the sensitive approach, try Dr. Phil.

"I don't cater to kids," he said. "I don't have prima donnas or hot dogs or mustaches or earrings. I'm old school—have fun and compete like hell. The greatest compliment I've heard about our program is that Indiana kids get better."

If improvement means running an extra mile or two to ensure the Hoosiers do things right the first time, Morgan won't hesitate. For instance, there was the time he ordered wind sprints in the aftermath of a poorly played home loss to Valparaiso. The Crusaders chuckled as they headed to their vans.

"Coach is very intense," said Ryan Smith, a relief pitcher on the 2003 team. "He's a perfectionist. He knows things aren't ever going to be perfect all the time, but that's what he demands. That's what we strive for—to be perfect. When it doesn't happen, he takes it personal."

Added Corby Heckman, all-Big Ten second baseman in 2003: "He wants everything done the right way the first time. He's very attentive to detail."

When those details aren't met, Morgan chews rump with the best of them. Ryan Smith, who wrapped up his five-year career in the spring of 2003, endured his share of tirades.

"He gets on us a lot," he said. "After being here five years, something you realize is he's not being mean, that he's trying to make you better. It's made me better. I came in immature. After five years I'm leaving more of a man. I can attribute all that to playing here and playing for Coach. I don't think things would have been the same with a coach who wasn't so hard nosed and wanting things done right."

Morgan doesn't coddle players. The best get as good as the worst, although Mickey Morandini, a three-time all-Big Ten performer in the 1980s, insisted his former coach has mellowed.

"But he's still a hard-nosed, very aggressive coach," Morandini said. "That's why Indiana has been so productive over the years. He gets the most out of his players."

The key, said 1992 Triple Crown winner Mike Smith, is to focus on the message and not the delivery.

"He pushes you mentally and physically," he said. "He pushes discipline. He doesn't care if you're the All-American. If the bus leaves at 8:30 and you show up at 8:31, you're finding a way to the park."

Mike Smith remembered a game against Stetson his freshman year. He was the starting third baseman as the Hoosiers opened the season with an 11-0 record. They'd just returned from their spring trip and were looking for more against an unheralded visitor. But they trailed 3-2 entering the ninth inning when, with two runners on base, Smith came to the plate with instructions to bunt. He tried and popped out to the catcher.

"Coach went bananas on me," Smith said. "I was almost crying, just because I didn't get a bunt down. Needless to say, the next time I got the bunt down and advanced the runner."

Morandini, who played 10 years in the majors, endured some of the same blistering lessons.

"He was a very intense coach," he said. "Probably the most intense coach I ever played for."

Including the majors?

"You can't be intense in the majors," Morandini said with a laugh. "The players run the teams now."

Morgan doesn't pull punches—starting with his recruiting pitch.

"I tell kids I not only expect their best, I demand it. That's not easy. I won't lower the bar for anybody. I care enough about my kids to get on them. It's tough love and they have to take it in that perspective."

Perspective often comes best at the end of a career.

"It's been hard playing here," Ryan Smith said. "It's been the hardest thing I've done in my life. He said that on my recruiting trip. He probably tells everybody that—that it will be the hardest thing you've done in your life. And it was. But it was still a great five years."

Scrambling Mo

If you understand nothing else about Bob Morgan, understand this—he throws batting practice. Rain, snow, hail, line drives off his shoulder, shattered fingers, bruised back, it doesn't matter. He will throw and to hell with the consequences.

"During batting practice he was Mr. Tough Guy," Mike Smith said. "I remember one time he took a line shot to the shoulder. He got lit up. He acted like he didn't get hit, but I knew deep down he was just dying. I was in the cage laughing. He stayed out there and kept throwing. He wanted to set the example that you're not going to knock me out."

"Yeah, I've been hit many times," Morgan said. "I've had big dots on my back where I've been hit. Several times I've been hit so hard, I thought I digested the ball."

Jeff Calcaterra has heard all the batting practice stories and embellished many.

"Coach is notorious for throwing batting practice all the time and for throwing it hard," he said. "He's right up on you, about 40 feet, sometimes 35. I don't know if it's the adrenaline, but he chucks it in there so that it seems like it's 90 to 95 mph."

Players tested Morgan's tough-guy posture by rocketing line drives off the protective screen in front of him.

"One of his nicknames is Mojo," Calcaterra said, "so we had what we'd call a Scramble Mo. We tried to hit it as hard as we could off the screen. Coach was so close he didn't have time to react. He'd do this body gyration. We'd keep track on the chalkboard in the locker room how many guys scrambled Mo. You focused on hitting, but whenever you could scream one back at him, you did. That was our goal."

Achieving that goal sometimes produced unexpected consequences. For instance Doug Whatmore, a pitcher from 1989 to 1991, faced Morgan's wrath.

"Doug was a big left-handed pitcher," Calcaterra said. "He was a wrestler from Toledo. Now he's a cop. Back then he looked like an offensive lineman.

"Coach was pitching and one guy scrambled him. The ball got through the corner of the screen and caught him in the ribs. You could hear him go, 'EEEEE!' It was like all his breath left him. Doug had been handing him balls. When he got hit, Doug grabbed him and asked him if he was all right. Because of Coach's ego to not let anyone know he was hurt, he started climbing all over Doug about handing him the balls. He just jumped all over him. We were rolling."

Morgan knows players sometime target him.

"That's great because they're hitting it up the middle," he said. "That's where you want to hit it. I don't get mad. The only time I do is if they aren't hitting the ball well, if they are out in front of pitches or miss a hit and run and don't hit it on the ground. Then I heat them up a little. I don't say much. I throw one by them or throw a nasty deuce (curveball) to get the message across."

And that message comes every day.

"Players think I'm the bionic man," Morgan said. "But if you get your arm in shape and you have good mechanics, you can do it every day."

Not even cold weather deters Morgan, a former all-Mid-American Conference pitcher for Ohio University who pitched in the Detroit Tigers' organization in the late 1960s.

"I remember as a freshman going to Iowa," Mike Smith said. "They had a stud pitcher named Cal Eldred (who later pitched in the majors for Milwaukee and the Chicago White Sox). It's 19 degrees and snowing and we have to face a guy throwing 90 mph. It was too cold to have batting practice at the park, so we went to the hotel parking lot and Coach threw batting practice with plastic golf balls."

Calcaterra remembered another cold Iowa trip.

"It was around 1990 and it was frigid. It was like 40 below with the wind chill. We're on the bus and supposed to take batting practice. It was so cold, Coach just had two guys out at a time, one to hit and one to feed him balls. It's like the second group out there and Coach gets drilled right in the back. He threw down the balls and said, 'That's it.' Four guys got to hit and that was the end of batting practice."

Mickey Morandini's most memorable batting practice incident came when Morgan took a line drive to his glove hand during a spring trip to Florida.

"It broke his finger and he shook it off and kept throwing," Morandini said. "The next day his finger was bent in about six different places. It was one of the ugliest things I've ever seen, but he continued to throw."

Added Morgan: "When we finished B.P., the trainer was afraid to come to the mound. It was like, just leave Coach alone. Well, he finally comes up to me and says, 'Coach, let me see your finger.' Then it was, 'Coach, we have to go to the doctor.' I said, 'We're playing in 15 minutes. We'll go to the doctor when we get back to Bloomington.'"

The problem—that would be in another week.

"The trainer says, 'Coach.' I said, 'Maybe you didn't hear me. I'm not going to the doctor.'"

Morgan paid the consequences.

"Because of my hard-headedness, the finger sets in. Now I go to the doctor and he sends me to a hand specialist. I had to get a pin in it. It hurt so bad that year, I almost used to cry in the shower. It would be aching like you couldn't imagine."

Morgan, of course, never let his players see his pain.

"I try to be an image for them as far as mental toughness. What I ask them to do I expect from myself."

Even in his mid-50s, those expectations continue.

"I was a pitcher and I like the workout. I'm in shape enough I can pitch an hour to the guys every day. And I think I throw good batting practice. I want to help my kids get better. I enjoy it when they hit the ball hard."

Keeping It Fun

Times might change, Calcaterra said, but personalities don't.

"It seems that each four to five years we have the same personalities. I don't know that we're consciously recruiting that, but you get the guy who is kind of a sicko, the guy who's a jokster, the hard-nosed guy, the grandpa figure who takes care of guys, the convicts and the geeks who are brainiacs and can't figure out how to cover first base."

A practical joke from Calcaterra's days involved freshmen and the practice schedule. Morgan would post the schedule in the morning with the mandate that everybody showed up for practice in uniform. Veteran Phil Dauphin would take the schedule and add a note that all freshmen should report in T-shirts and shorts.

"All the upper classmen would be wearing shorts in the locker room before practice," Calcaterra said. "The freshmen would come in, see us, see the note, and put on shorts and T-shirts. Then they'd go to practice early because they wanted to impress Coach Morgan. After they left, we put on our practice pants and uniforms and headed to the field."

"When the freshmen showed up, Coach went livid because they were supposed to be in uniforms. Then he'd see us and get a chuckle. He knew we'd gotten them."

Another practical joke at the freshmen's expense involved a veteran player calling them on the phone after they'd had a good game. Marty Wolfe, who played in the early 1990s, was notorious for calling newcomers while pretending to be a student newspaper reporter.

"He'd say the paper wanted a photo and that the player needed to show up in a suit and tie and meet in the student union," Calcaterra said. "So he'd show up and half the team would be there to razz him. Stuff like that kept us loose. Those were the things that made it fun."

The Recruiting Scene

Morgan, like his coaching predecessors, faces the Midwest recruiting disadvantage of winter that sends many of the best players south. He targets the state of Indiana and the surrounding states, although the Hoosiers have signed players out of Maryland and Virginia.

"I stay in the Midwest and try to be realistic," he said. "Baseball is not an equal playing field. And until we get a common starting date and can play through the summer, it won't be."

Schools are allowed 22 weeks of practice and 56 games over a calendar year. There is no designated starting date for games. Southern schools, because of the warm weather advantage, get earlier starts.

"If you have a common starting date," Morgan said, "and if you can't start until April 1 and play through June, with the College World Series in July, then I have a better chance to get the better players."

The Hoosiers have the NCAA-maximum 11.7 scholarships for a 32-player roster. Scholarships are divided to maximize the money. One player might get a 60 percent scholarship, another 30, and so forth.

"It's like a puzzle you try to mix and match," Calcaterra said. "And if a school offers a kid 30 percent and we really want him, we might offer 35 percent."

Full ride offers are rare and usually come to dominating pitchers.

"The kid would have to be an absolute stud," Calcaterra said.

Morgan said he once didn't go after the best players because of attitude concerns. Now, he's less selective.

"In the past we didn't go after the super studs maybe as much as we should have," he said. "Maybe they were spoiled, maybe they were prima donnas. I won't put up that. But I've changed in the last 10 years or so because the game has changed.

"When I first started coaching you could out-coach people. You could out-work them. You can still do that a little bit. But you can't have a zoo without the animals. It's all about recruiting now. I'd say 75 percent, maybe 80 percent of the profession is getting the players. I've seen guys who aren't very good coaches have great programs. Why? Because they have great players. So now we go after those super studs. Let's get the best kids, the best talent, the best student-athletes, and let me worry about whether they can take the discipline and work ethic."

Long-term Success

Morgan made instant impact after arriving following successful stops at Wooster and Kent State. IU won a school-record 44 games in his first season of 1984, and then upped it to 57 in 1985. But Big Ten success was tougher to achieve and it wasn't until 1991 that the Hoosiers had a winning league record. They were 15-12-1 in 1991, 15-12 in '93. Their best conference record came in 1996, when they were 18-8 to finish second in the regular season standings.

"The '85 team had a lot of very good hitters," Morgan said. "Danny Winters and Billy Mueller were the best catching-DH combination in the Big Ten that year. Barry Jones pitched in the big leagues. But we just didn't have enough depth. We had five or six really good players, and after that it really dropped off."

Morgan has had only one losing season. In 2001, IU went 24-31. The Hoosiers bounced back to make the Big Ten tourney in 2002 and 2003.

Morgan's favorite team isn't the '85 or '96 squads, but the 1993 group that went 38-21 overall and qualified for the conference tourney.

"We weren't very talented, but we were a good team," Morgan said. "We had great leadership. They gave me everything they possibly could."

Catcher Dave Snedden and outfielder Joe Sturtz led that team. They are on Morgan's list of all-time toughest players.

"Snedden was a catcher so tough, he stayed here for three years as a backup," Morgan said. "But by the time he was a senior he played as well as any catcher I've had. He was tough. Nasty. He got hit with bats. Hit with balls. He was just beat up and he never gave in. We made the (tournament) because of his leadership and toughness.

"Sturtz was a great leader and a great player. He decided in his junior and senior years that, 'I'm a marginal player. I have to bust my butt to be on this team and start on this team, and I'm going to do it.' His job was to get on base and he did. He set a record that year with 62 walks."

The only no-hitter of the Morgan era came on March 23, 1984, when Bob Hicks shut down Wabash 2-1. Hicks struck out 14 and walked two in seven innings.

However, if Morgan could have one pitcher return to pitch one big game, it would be Bob Scafa. The left hander had four shutout victories in 1993. He won seven games that season and had a 2.15 earned run average.

"He was in such a rhythm that year," Morgan said. "You could almost just sit in the dugout and watch him work. He had a sneaky fastball, probably a mid-80 mph guy. He had a good curve and a good change. He'd work it in and out. He kept guys off stride. He was not overpowering, but he pitched with a lot of confidence."

The Legacy

Weeks of recruiting and working summer camps are reflected in Morgan's tanned face as he relaxes in his Assembly Hall office. The 1996 Big Ten tourney championship trophy rests on his desk. Behind him is a plaque commemorating his 1,000th career victory.

"When I first came here, I could tell there was not a lot of commitment to baseball," he said. "People didn't have answers to a lot of things. Their heads were in the woods a little bit as far as baseball was concerned. They'd say, 'Geez, the other coach didn't want it. Why do you want it now?' They didn't understand that there are some things you need.

"It hasn't been easy. Indiana wasn't very good in baseball. We've made it to where we're competitive year in and year out. There's a lot of pride in the program."

Criticism has occasionally surfaced about non-conference schedules that lack the quality teams necessary to challenge for Big Ten supremacy. But Morgan schedules with what he calls "a smart" approach. He doesn't see the benefits of playing southern powerhouses with advantages in outside practice and early season games that northern schools can't match. So while he has played strong schools during spring break trips—sweeping three straight from Tulane when it was a top-10 team in 1997, losing to Oklahoma State in 1998 and 2000, and to Oklahoma in 1991—he has shied away from such powers as Texas, Miami, and Louisiana State.

In recent years the Hoosiers have mixed spring trip games with such fellow northern schools as Northern Illinois, Seton Hall, Bowling Green, Pittsburgh and Kansas State, with lesser-known opponents as Marist, Quinnipiac, Drexel, Yale, and Farleigh Dickinson.

"A lot of schools do this," Morgan said. "You go to Florida, say Bradenton, and whoever is there when you're there, that's who you get matched up with. You're playing teams from the same climate with the same disadvantages, so it's more of an equalizer. Before if you went to Florida, you got your head handed to you. Southern schools would offer you $4,000 and pay for your hotel rooms. They'd have played like 20 games and you're just coming out of the gym. Basically, they want some snowbirds to come down and beat up on.

"Now, we're trying to be a little smarter."

And Morgan has been smart. You don't win more than 1,000 games and not be. And if the victories didn't produce a shelf full of conference championship trophies, they did result in something longer lasting.

"You always like to win a few more championships, a few more games, but the real value is not the wins and losses, but the relationships you develop," he said. "And we've won our share. We have a program that has a lot of class and pride and respect."

Morgan said he could see himself coaching six to eight more years, which would put him into his early 60s. He's less certain about matching the longevity of 67-year-old Rice coach Wayne Graham, who won the 2003 college World Series.

"I don't know if I can make that," he said. "I'd like to coach as long as I enjoy it. As long as I still have the energy and still have high expectations and demands I can do myself. I'm a hands-on guy. I get involved. I throw B.P.. I hit infield. I do the same thing in my camps. Coach Morgan is out there with the infielders. He's demonstrating. He's working right there with them. As long as I can do that, I'll continue coaching."

And when he can't continue, how would he like to be remembered?

"As a very hard worker who was an outstanding coach and who really cared about his kids. I want my legacy to be that he was a guy who was a very tough coach who gave his kids tough love. A guy who had high expectations and wasn't willing to accept less than your best. A guy who taught that toughness is an asset and not a liability."

The Hoosiers set the school's all-time record for victories in a season when they went 57-19-1 in 1985. No other IU squad has won more than 44 games in a season. Indiana hit .344 as a team while recording a 4.04 earned run average. Key contributors that season were (left to right) Mike Humphrey, Chris Sigler, Bill Mueller, Bruce Morrison and coach Bob Morgan. Humphrey won 10 games that season. Mueller set a then school record with 23 home runs. Sigler stole a team-leading 29 bases. Morrison hit .348.

In 1985, Indiana got off to a 22-4 start. Most of the victories were blowouts, including 31-0 over Savannah State, 17-3 over Bellarmine and 22-11 over Bethune-Cookman. The Hoosiers had a tougher time in the Big Ten, finishing 8-8. Pictured from that team are (left to right) Mike Ramsey, Chris Sigler, Brad Fella, Pat Crews, and coach Bob Morgan.

Pitcher Eric Sieber won 13 games from 1987 to 1990 with a career 5.25 earned run average. He led the team in innings pitched twice, with 69.1 in 1987 and 70.2 in 1989. He tied for the team lead in victories with Eric Jacques in 1989. Both won six games.

Scott Zimmerman was tough to beat in 1987. He went 6-1 with a 4.96 earned run average, mainly because his control was so good. He struck out 50 while walking only 19 in 61.2 innings.

When coach Bob Morgan had a big game in the early 1990s, he turned to pitcher Bob Scafa. In 1991, Scafa started a school-record eight Big Ten games. He started seven in 1992, '93 and '94. He threw an IU record four shutouts in conference action in 1993, and then added another Big Ten shutout in 1994. His 111 strikeouts in Big Ten games is the school career record.

Phil Dauphin ranks just behind Mickey Morandini as the top home run-base stealing threat in school history. Dauphin's 29 career home runs rank ninth. His 57 stolen bases rank eighth. He also drove in 178 runs, which ranks fifth on the IU all-time list. He set a school record with 12 triples in 1989.

While Bob Scafa was coach Bob Morgan's choice to start big games in the early 1990s, Chris Koehler was often his choice to finish them. Koehler's eight career Big Ten saves rank second in school history to Chris Wilson's 11. Koehler appeared in 36 conference games, the school record.

Coach Bob Morgan could count on Dan Winters (center) and Alex Smith to come through with the big hits in the mid 1980s. Winters was a career .348 hitter while slugging 18 home runs. Smith's .393 career average is the second highest in school history.

Alex Smith's home run trot was a familiar sight to Indiana fans in the mid-1980s. He set a then school record with 43 career home runs. He added another school mark—since broken—with 223 runs batted in.

Phil Dauphin was a practical joker along with being an All-Big Ten caliber player. He targeted freshmen, convincing them to attend practice in shorts and T-shirts instead of uniforms. His best year was 1990 when he led IU in hitting (.368), stolen bases (23), walks (39), runs batted in (52), home runs (13) and hits (70).

Kevin Goins was a .299 career hitter in the early 1990s. He hit 14 home runs and 32 doubles in his three-year career with 85 runs batted in. He led the Hoosiers with 34 walks in 1992.

When it came to winning Big Ten games, no Hoosier pitcher did it better than Steve Schaefer. He has the school record for conference victories, with 13. He also ranks second in league innings pitched (155) and games started (28), and is tied with Bob Scafa and Dan Ferrell in complete games. All three had 12.

Bob Scafa compiled a 22-15 record from 1991to 1994 with a 4.38 ERA. He ranks third in school history with 229 strikeouts, trailing only Eric Jacques (244) and Brian Partenheimer (235). In 1993 Scafa was named all-conference, the first Hoosier pitcher to be so honored since Paul Michaels in 1960. He signed with the Los Angeles Dodgers, but never made it to the majors. He also never made much money. While pitching for Class A Yakima in 1994, he made $850 a month.

Eric Jacques set the strikeout standard for Indiana. The hard-throwing lefthander struck out 244 batters from 1986 to 1989 while winning 23 games.

Steve Schaefer compiled a 23-17 career record from 1990 to 1993 with a 4.86 ERA.

Eric Jacques was the IU workhorse in 1989, when he set a school record for appearances in a season, with 30. He was responsible for 32 victories in his career with 23 wins and nine saves.

Brian Harris set the school record for stolen bases in a season in 1997. He had 50 that year, including four against IU Southeast. He finished with 67 steals in his two-year career.

Pitcher Brad Partenheimer was a big part of IU's run to a Big Ten tourney championship and NCAA Tournament appearance in 1996. He is the school's career leader for conference innings pitched (156.2) and ranks second in Big Ten victories (12). He struck out 104 conference hitters to rank second in school history.

Rich Vozel could handle the load academically and athletically in the early 1990s. He was a three-time member of the Big Ten all-academic team. As a player he hit .252 for his career with 22 doubles and 59 runs batted in. He has the Hoosiers' two best sacrifice totals, getting a record 15 in 1992 and 13 in '91.

Doug Devore earned first-team All-Big Ten honors in 1999 after leading IU with 72 hits, 15 doubles, 19 home runs and 65 runs batted in. He also led the team with 150 total bases and a .750 slugging percentage.

Dan Haegele was an All-America player for Indiana in the late 1990s. He finished among the school career leaders in Big Ten play in hits (111) and runs (79), ranking second to Mike Smith (132 hits, 87 runs) in both categories. Haegele's knack of crowding the plate caused painful consequences. He was hit by pitches seven times in 1999, the school record.

With men on base, Blake St. Clair was a clutch performer. From 1998 to 2001 he drove in 126 runs and had a career batting average of .310.

Davis Ferris was a pitching mainstay from 1998 to 2001. He had a career record of 12-6 and struck out 140 batters. He led the team in earned run average in 2000 with a 3.75 ERA. His 35 earned runs allowed also led the team. His 10 strikeouts against Indiana Wesleyan in 2000 set the Sembower Field record.

Blake St. Clair saved his best for last, dominating the IU offensive statistics as a senior in 2001. He led the team in hits (66), doubles (12), triples (4), runs batted in (51), total bases (107) and walks (36).

Chris Wilson is the IU career saves record holder. He totaled 15 from 1997 to 2000. His eight saves in 1999 were the school record until Ryan Smith broke it with nine in 2002.

Eric Blakeley earned academic All-Big Ten honors in 2000 and 2001. He finished with a career batting average of .310 with 14 home runs and 116 runs batted in. He also had 35 steals.

The 2002 Hoosiers ranked 12th in the nation in hitting with a .330 team average. That helped them finish fourth in the Big Ten and qualify for the conference tourney for the first time since 1996.

Kennard Jones played just one year at Indiana and made it count. He was the Big Ten tri-player of the year after hitting .411 with 22 stolen bases in 2002. He played at Wallace State Junior College his first two years. He was a third-round choice of the San Diego Padres and made the Class A All-Star game in 2003 while with the Fort Wayne Wizards.

Pitcher Nick Vitielliss was a second-team all-Big Ten choice in 2002 after going 8-1 with a 3.58 ERA. He tied IU's single-season record for conference wins with five. He made a big jump after going just 3-3 in his first two seasons with a 4.75 ERA.

Eric Blakeley was drafted by the Seattle Mariners in 2002 after a senior season in which he hit .330 with 10 home runs and 60 runs batted in. Playing for the Everett AquaSox of the Shortseason Northwest League in 2003, Blakeley hit .300 with three homers and 15 runs batted in.

Gibran Hamdan was a two-sport athlete for the Hoosiers. As a senior first baseman in 2002 he hit .335 with six home runs and 38 runs batted in. He finished with career numbers of .297 average, 10 home runs and 72 runs batted in. Hamdan spent his first four football seasons (including a redshirt year) behind Antwaan Randle El at quarterback. In 2002, with Randle El moving on to the NFL, Hamdan and Tommy Jones shared the starting quarterback job. Hamdan did well enough to sign as a free agent with the Washington Redskins.

Ryan Smith ranks as one of the top relief pitchers in Indiana history. As a junior in 2002 he set a school record with nine saves. He compiled a 3-2 record that year with a 3.06 earned run average. As a senior he went 4-1 with a 4.39 ERA. He had five saves.

Corby Heckman came into his own as a sophomore in 2003. He hit .372 with 15 doubles and 29 RBIs to earn all-conference honors. Not bad for someone who batted just seven times as a freshman.

Nick Evans capped a solid career in 2003 by hitting .321 with 40 RBIs. He led the team in hitting as a sophomore (.359), then came back to hit .333 as a junior.

Jacob Cary emerged as the IU ace in 2003. Pitching against the top teams on the schedule, he went 7-3 with a 5.40 ERA. He had a team-leading 49 strikeouts. He was an academic all-conference selection.

At 6-foot-6 and 210 pounds, Chris Behrens was an intimidating factor on the mound. As a junior in 2003 he went 5-4 with a 4.50 ERA and totaled 42 strikeouts. He was a middle reliever as a sophomore and compiled a 6.30 ERA with no decisions. As a freshman in 2001 he went 3-1 with a 4.94 ERA and 28 strikeouts in 27 innings.

Senior Kevin O'Brien finished unbeaten on the mound in 2003 with a 4-0 record and a 4.58 ERA. He started his career as a catcher, hitting .203 as a freshman and .197 as a sophomore. Because of his strong arm, he was moved to pitcher as a junior. He went 1-0 with a 4.24 ERA as a middle reliever in 2002.

Josh Lewis made instant impact as a freshman in 2003, compiling a 5-2 record with a 4.55 ERA. A native of Maryland, he was part of the Hoosiers' recent East Coast recruiting efforts.

Who says good fielding doesn't pay off? Shortstop Seth Bynum combined outstanding defense and solid hitting to get drafted in the 38th round by the Montreal Expos in 2003. Bynum hit .287 with nine doubles and 34 runs batted in. That was his first season as a Hoosier after playing his first two years at Lincoln Trail Community College in Kentucky.

Doug Devore ranks fourth on IU's all-time single season home run list. He hit 19 in 1999. He finished with 28 to rank 10th in school history. He played in the Arizona Diamondbacks organization. The outfielder hit .293 with nine home runs and 55 runs batted in for AAA Tucson of the Pacific Coast League in 2003.

TEN

Future Stadium

The proposed future of Indiana baseball has the retro feel so popular in the sport these days. It will have limestone and lights, covered seats, locker rooms, offices and so much more. It will be a stadium and not a field.

If it ever gets built.

Coach Bob Morgan said the university has about half of the funding for the proposed $5 million stadium, part of an athletic complex that would also include softball and field hockey fields. Plans call for it to be built near the state police post on what is now intramural fields just north of the tennis complex. Morgan said he hopes the baseball stadium is built by 2007.

"The sooner the better. If we wait another year, and then another year before it happens, we fall further behind."

Sooner will probably mean later according to athletic director Terry Clapacs, focused on eliminating a $3 million deficit that surfaced in 2002.

"A baseball stadium is something on our long-term plan," he said. "It's not on the horizon any time in the next couple of years that's for sure. We would need to raise the money to do it. We really haven't started. We have other priority issues that are ahead of that in terms of fund raising. So it's long term. It's not something that is active at the moment."

When it becomes active, Clapacs added, it would be done right.

"We'd want it to be on a par with the other Big Ten baseball stadiums. It can be done very nicely. And having a well-designed, attractive baseball stadium would add a certain character to the athletic district."

In these cutthroat recruiting times, you look for an edge everywhere, and facilities play a major role, especially when you lack the southern schools' warm-weather allure.

"Sembower Field hurts us in recruiting," assistant coach Jeff Calcaterra said. "You look at the grandstands as bleachers that have been there for 40 years. Yeah, we've got new dugouts, a new press box and a new scoreboard, but that's basically the only improvement in the 15 years I've been here. Little league fields had better scoreboards than what we had. It was way overdue.

"If we add a five or six million dollar stadium, with lights and the whole shebang, we'd be able to entice the players in our region who now go to the Clemsons and Vanderbilts and the other southern schools. That would make our level rise to where we could compete at a national level. I'm not saying we'd win a national championship, but we could compete with Ohio State and Minnesota every year for a Big Ten championship."

IU baseball coaches said the program needs that kind of financial commitment.

"It depends how serious the administration is about baseball," Calcaterra said. "We know basketball and football are No. 1 and No. 2 here. We're probably fourth or fifth."

University officials are focused on raising funds to upgrade Memorial Stadium and the football program. A new artificial surface was added in the summer of 2003. Clapacs is committed to enclosing the north end of Memorial Stadium with an office complex.

"That will take priority," he said.

Former IU coach and player Bob Lawrence said he first broached the subject about building a new baseball stadium in the 1970s.

"I said 30 years ago they should put it by the state police station," he said. "That's where I wanted it so we could have more parking. I said the intramural fields should be where Sembower is, right where the dorms are. But they didn't listen. Instead, they put in the intramural fields by the police station."

Clapacs said he is listening now.

"Sembower Field is a nice little stadium, but it's just in the wrong location. We'd like to have the baseball stadium and women's softball venue in the athletic district on [the north] side of 17th Street."

That's good news for those associated with the program.

"I realize for that to happen it takes money and that money has to be here at a certain time," said Ryan Smith, a relief pitcher on the 2003 team. "In the future it looks like that will happen. I wish I could be here when it does."

So does 1992 Triple Crown winner Mike Smith.

"When I saw a picture of the future of baseball at Indiana, I was happy about it," he said. "It's needed. For a Big Ten school, well, the Sembower Field surface is one of the nicest ones in the conference, but the overall stadium feel isn't the greatest."

An improved stadium feel, Lawrence said, would boost the program.

"It would be a big addition. The location would be better, the parking would be better, you'd get better crowds and it would add a lot to the recruiting."

Added Mickey Morandini: "Sembower was a great field for me, but that was 20 years ago. Stadiums have come a long way since then."

Recruits notice, Morgan said.

"You need to show a commitment from the university," he said. "You're able to recruit with that commitment. I like our location now because it's by the dorms. It integrates the campus with athletes. Kids can fall out of their dorm room and be on the baseball field. But if moving out there means having a new facility, let's go. I'd like to coach in the new stadium before I go. I'd like to have an office out there. I'd like to coach under the lights. If we got it I'd feel like I'd died and gone to heaven."

There She Blows

There is no truth to the rumor that the jet stream blows over Sembower Field.

"If the wind was going to blow anywhere in Monroe County," Lawrence said, "it was going to blow there. It seemed like the wind was blowing all the time."

The advantage flip-flops between pitchers and hitters.

"One day the wind is blowing out, the next day it's blowing in," said Corby Heckman, an All-Big Ten second baseman on the 2003 team. "If it's blowing in, hitters don't have a chance to hit it out. If the wind is blowing out, well, it's not a big park, so it can be extremely hitter friendly."

Ryan Smith knew that friendliness all too well.

"As a pitcher it was kind of scary knowing balls could fly out pretty easy," he said.

Lawrence felt that fear as a coach and reaped the benefits as a player.

"If it was a cold day, the wind was coming out of the north, so it was blowing in," he said. "On a warm day, it was from the south, which meant it was blowing out. That was a hitter's paradise."

Paradise came in isolation for Sembower Field's first decade. While Jordan Field (used for the first half of the 20th Century) was in the center of campus near what is now the Memorial Union, Sembower was built in 1951 at the center of nothing. Fee Lane was a road through farmland. Surrounding dormitories were years from existence.

"There was nothing around it then," Lawrence said. "It was the farthest thing north on campus. McNutt and Foster and those dorms weren't there. Just fields. Where Assembly Hall is now was a farm."

Sembower Field was built because Jordan Field had out-lived its usefulness. It was never a true baseball facility, having also been used for football and track. And spring flooding was an annual problem.

"Getting Sembower was a big deal," former coach and player Ernie Andres said. "You can't imagine playing baseball in Jordan Field. It was unique, but it wasn't ideal. Having a regular baseball field was a big step."

That step required a long walk.

"We dressed at the H.P.E.R. and walked up to the field," Lawrence said.

Sembower Field in those years had plenty of parking, something that is no longer the case. But plenty of parking didn't mean plenty of fans. Unlike Jordan Field, which drew 4,000 or more for big games, crowds rarely reached 1,000 at Sembower.

"We'd get maybe 600 to 700 people," Lawrence said.

The crowds haven't changed much over the years, but the playing surface has. Bob Morgan and his staff put in countless hours to ensure the field is as good as any in the league.

"Coach took great pride in the grass being straight and the stones being in place," 1992 Triple Crown winner Mike Smith said. "He led by example. You'd see him out there picking up stones. He's committed to it, just like he's committed to the whole program."

It's a commitment as strong now as it was when the University Baseball Club formed 1867. Because then, as now, at Indiana University, baseball matters.

Sembower Field is named for Charles Jacob Sembower, a long-time IU professor of English who was a Hoosier second baseman from 1891 to 1894. When the facility was built in the early 1950s, it was well north of the existing campus. Now it is in the middle of one of the busiest locations on campus, next to Foster Quadrangle and across from McNutt and Briscoe residence hall complexes. Designed as a hitter friendly park, it is 380 feet to center, 365 feet to right center and 370 feet to left center. Its aluminum seating has a capacity of 3,000.

After more than half a century of use, Sembower Field (left, next to softball field) has been host to plenty of impressive achievements. For instance, the record for most runs batted in for a single game is 10 by Byron Bradley against Tri-State in 1992. Mike Smith drove in nine against Wisconsin-Milwaukee that same season. Bradley set the record for total bases in a game (17), also against Tri-State in 1992. That included a record four home runs. Two Hoosiers have gone 5-for-5 in a game at Sembower—Robert Crotty against Indianapolis in 1995 and Dan Haegele against Penn State in 1998. Only five times has an IU pitcher thrown for nine innings at Sembower and Kyle Boyd did it three times in the 1997 and '98 seasons. The rest of the athletic complex, including Memorial Stadium and Assembly Hall, can be seen from this view.

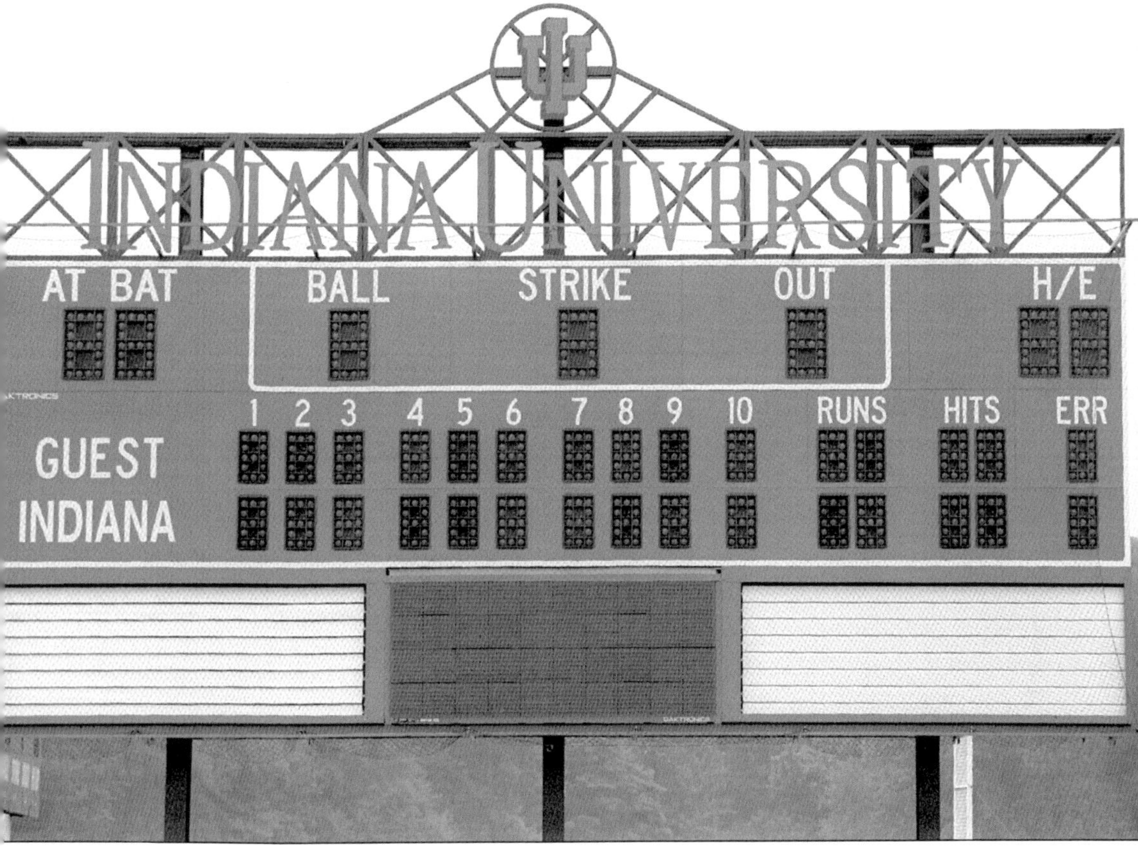

This retro-style scoreboard was installed in 1996 and was a big improvement from the 1950s-era scoreboard that had been in use for most of Sembower Field's existence. That was one of several additions made 1996. Others included a new underground sprinkler system, foam padding on the backstop and the outfield walls, and new fencing around the outfield and backstop areas.

Just because Indiana is the Big Ten's southern-most school doesn't mean it gets a winter reprieve. And when the weather turns cold and snowy and nasty, the Hoosiers utilize their indoor facilities. In 1990 that meant the Fieldhouse, the indoor track venue and former basketball home. Catcher Jeff Calcaterra (above) took advantage that season to help work the pitchers' arms into shape. The Hoosiers needed all the help they could get. Their 5.44 earned run average was the worst of the Bob Morgan era up to that point, a major factor in their 30-27-1 record. However, their 14-14 Big Ten mark was a major improvement from their 5-23 showing of the previous year. The team no longer works out in the Fieldhouse, now know as the Gladstein Indoor Track & Field Fieldhouse. Instead, it utilizes the Mellencamp Pavilion.